KNITTING starting STITCHES

Lyric Books Limited

© 1993 Lyric Books Limited,
66B The Broadway, Mill Hill, London NW7 3TF, England

First published in 1993

ISBN 0 7111 0081 0

Printed in Belgium by
Proost International Book Production

Series Consultant: Eleanor Van Zandt

Art Editor: Stefanie Paradine

Production Editor: Monika York

CONTENTS

Introduction   4

1 First Steps ...

Knitting Equipment   6
Yarn   7
Holding Needles and Yarn   8
Casting On   9
Basic Stitches   11
Basic Fabrics   12
Casting Off   13
Correcting Mistakes   14
Simple Shaping   16
Joining in a New Yarn   17
Decorative Techniques   18
Working from a Pattern   20
Picking Up Stitches   22
Joining the Seams   23
Abbreviations and Symbols   24

2 Easy does it ...

Basic Fabrics   26
Simple Textures   28
Scarf   30
All-over Textures   32
Cushions   36

3 Child's play ...

All-over Patterns   44
Child's T-Shirt   48
Baby's Blanket   52
Slip Stitch Patterns   54

4 Go for bold ...

Textured Patterns   60
Woman's Sweater and Skirt   64
Man's Cabled Sweater   72
Cable Stitches   74

Introduction

As every knitter knows, knitting is not just a craft, it is a passion. Once you learn to knit you will almost always have a project under way, to pick up while chatting with a friend or watching television, or to take with you to while away a long journey.

STARTING STITCHES will show you just how enjoyable knitting can be. The book is really three books in one: a guide to basic knitting techniques, a collection of stitch patterns and a selection of projects.

All of the techniques required for the stitch patterns and projects are included in the 'First Steps' section. Text and illustrations show you (among other things) how to cast on and hold the yarn and needles, how to form the knit and purl stitches, how to shape the knitting and how to make up a finished garment. To make your knitting more exciting there are instructions for working slip stitch patterns and basic cables.

The stitch patterns range from simple knit and purl textures to slightly more ambitious patterns. They are given in both written and chart form - for those who find symbols easier to follow. Once you gain a little experience you will be able to substitute these stitches for the ones used in published patterns, or even use them in an original design of your own!

To begin with, however, we suggest that you practise your new skills by making some of the simple projects in this book. They include both garments and accessories, all specially designed to help you discover the pleasures of knitting.

KNITTING starting STITCHES

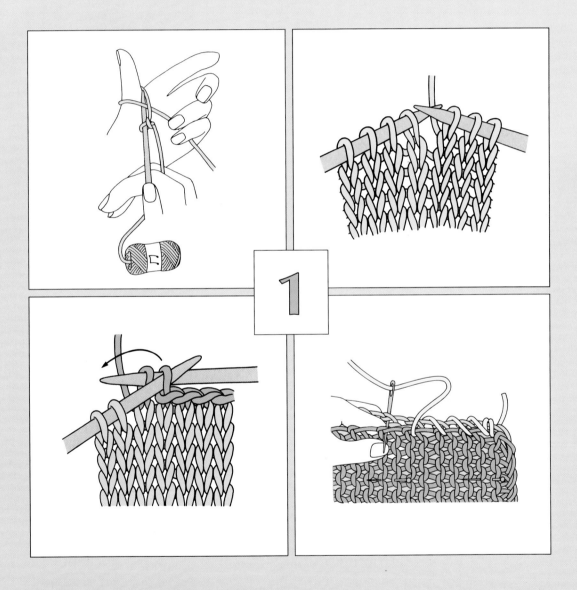

First Steps ...

Get to grips with your knitting with these foolproof instructions.

Knitting Equipment

Relatively little equipment is required for hand knitting. The main tools, of course, are the needles which you can acquire gradually in the course of working patterns calling for different sizes. In addition, you will sometimes need certain other items such as stitch holders and a large tapestry needle to complete a garment.

Pairs of knitting needles

These range in size from 2mm to 17mm in diameter (see conversion tables of those most commonly used) and are available in plastic, wood, bamboo, steel and aluminium. Choose the kind with which you can knit most comfortably and smoothly. They are also available in various lengths so use one that will hold the required number of stitches easily – stitches can easily fall off an overcrowded needle! Check that needles have nicely rounded points and are straight – blunt, bent or scratched needles all reduce the speed and efficiency of knitting.

Circular and double-pointed needles

These are used for knitting tubular, seamless fabric or for knitting flat rounds (such as circular shawls). Circular needles consist of two short needles joined by a length of flexible nylon and come in different lengths. Your pattern will usually tell you what length is required to accommodate the number of stitches comfortably. Circular needles can also be used like a pair of needles, turning at the end of each row wherever you have a large number of stitches, such as when knitting a large shawl.

Double-pointed needles are available in sets of four or (sometimes) five. They are often used to knit neckbands and can be used instead of a circular needle wherever the number of stitches is too small to reach around a circular needle. Double-pointed needles are also used for knitting seamless socks, gloves and berets.

Cable needles

These are short double-pointed needles which are used for holding stitches to the back or front of the work when moving stitches for a cable pattern (see page 19). They are generally available in three sizes. Use a size that will hold the stitches comfortably – neither stretching them nor slipping out. Cable needles with notches to hold the stitches are easier to use than the straight ones because the stitches do not slide off.

Stitch holders

These resemble large safety pins and are used to retain stitches that will be required later – for example across a pocket where the edging is done after the front is completed. Alternatively, thread a length of yarn through the stitches, slip them off the needle and knot both ends of the spare yarn together. Slip the stitches back on to a needle before knitting the edging.

Row counter

This is a cylindrical device with a dial used to record the number of rows knitted. Slip the row counter on to the end of one needle before starting to knit and turn the dial at the end of each row.

Tape measure

This is essential for measuring the length and width of the knitting, as well as for checking tension swatches (see page 20), although a ruler is more accurate for this.

Tapestry needle

This is a blunt-pointed needle which slips easily between the stitches and has a large eye for easy threading. Buy a large size. Do not use a sharp-pointed needle, as this will split the yarn.

Crochet hooks

These are useful for picking up dropped stitches (see page 15). Keep a selection of sizes appropriate for different thicknesses of yarn. Some knitted garments, especially baby clothes, have crocheted edges.

You will also need **dressmaker's pins**, preferably long ones with coloured heads which will not disappear in the knitting. These are used for pinning seams, for blocking and for marking tension swatches. **Safety pins** make ideal stitch holders for small numbers of stitches. They can also be used for holding dropped stitches and for marking button spacing. A small, sharp **pair of scissors** is another essential tool. A **needle gauge** may be useful for checking or converting needle sizes.

YARN

'Yarn' is the general term used for strands of fibre that are twisted (spun) together into a continuous thread. It encompasses both natural fibres and synthetic ones, as well as plain or fancy finishes and varying thicknesses and textures.

The range of yarns available is enormous, and new spinning techniques are constantly being developed to produce new effects.

Yarn thickness or weight

Yarns vary enormously in thickness (or weight) from very fine to very bulky – suitable for different types of knitting. Over the years a series of 'standard' or 'classic' yarn weights have been established. Those used in Britain and in other European countries are described below. However, the yarns available in each group are by no means identical, and the terms used signify merely a similarity in tension/gauge when knitted. Fancy yarns may also be available in these thicknesses but extra care should be taken if substituting one for a smooth yarn, to ensure that the correct tension/gauge is achieved.

2 ply and 3 ply

Until the 1950s these yarns were widely available and many old knitting

(Canadian) & UK Sizes	000	00	0	1	2	3	4	5	6	7	8	9	10	11	12	13	14
Metric Sizes (for UK)	10	9	8	7½	7	6½	6	5½	5	4½	4	3¾	3¼	3	2¾	2¼	2
US Sizes	15	13		11		10½	10	9	8	7	6	5	4	3	3	2	1	0

patterns using them can still be found. Nowadays, few people have the time or patience to work with very fine yarns and they are now used mainly for babies' garments. These yarns are available only in a limited range of colours, often only in white.

4 ply

This, too, is popular for baby clothes but is also used for adults' garments by knitters who are prepared to spend a little longer completing a garment. 4 ply is very effective for lacy garments and colour-patterned knitting, as it can achieve finer detail than is possible with thicker yarns. It is also very popular for crochet and machine knitting. It is available in a wide range of colours.

Double Knitting

By far the most popular of the standard yarns, double knitting can be used for babies', children's and adults' garments. Designs for double knitting range from light and lacy to plain and classic and to heavily textured and cabled garments. Double knitting is available in a vast range of colours and a variety of finishes.

Aran

Aran yarn (formerly also called triple) is generally used for heavily textured and cabled garments. Originally available only in a natural (cream) pure wool, it now comes in a wider range of colours, for fashion Aran-style knits and also in economical synthetic fibres. A traditional Aran knit in wool is extremely warm and durable.

Chunky

Quick to knit on large needles, chunky is especially popular with beginners. It is generally used for loose-fitting outdoor sweaters and jackets and can be plain or brushed. Most basic and current fashion shades are available, although the range is not as wide as for double knitting.

Yarn sources

The fibres from which yarn is spun can be of animal, vegetable or synthetic origin. Fibres are often combined, either for reasons of economy or to exploit the best qualities of each.

Wool is a popular fibre for hand knitting. It is warm and comfortable to wear and, because of its elasticity, pleasant to knit with. Another animal fibre, **mohair** (from the angora goat), is prized for its fluffy, luxurious texture; it is often combined with a synthetic fibre for extra strength. **Angora** (from the angora rabbit), **alpaca** and **cashmere** are other luxurious animal fibres.

Silk (from the silkworm) is the strongest and lightest of the natural fibres, although pure silk yarn containing many fibres, is dense and heavy. It takes dye very well, producing yarns in the richest range of colours. Silk is often combined with wool or mohair.

Cotton is a cool yarn, popular for summer garments and is now available in a variety of weights and finishes. Because of its non-elasticity it is somewhat difficult to knit with. This is even more true of **linen** which is normally mixed with other fibres to produce a more versatile yarn.

Synthetic or man-made fibres include **nylon**, **acrylic** and **viscose** (rayon). They are strong, hard wearing and often less expensive than natural fibres, but may lack the warmth and resilience of wool and the coolness of cotton or linen. However, they often combine well with natural fibres to produce economical, durable, yet attractive yarns.

Buying yarn

Yarn is most commonly sold wound into oblong balls which can be used as they are. Some yarn, particularly if it is very thick, may be sold in a coiled hank or skein. Yarn manufacturers (spinners) wrap each ball with a paper band printed with certain information, including the weight of the yarn (that is the number of grams or ounces in the ball), its fibre content (in percentages) and instructions for washing/dry cleaning and pressing. It may also state the ideal tension and recommended needle size.

Dye lot number Also given on the ball band are the shade number and a dye lot number. It is important to use yarn of the same dye lot for a single project. Different dye lots vary subtly in shade which may not be apparent when you are comparing two balls of yarn, but

will be very noticeable in a finished piece of knitting.

Always buy sufficient yarn of the same dye lot to complete the garment. If you do run out of yarn and cannot get any more from the shop, contact the spinner to see if there is any more available. Alternatively use the different dye lot for the edgings only, or work two rows alternately from each ball so that the change in shade is less noticeable.

American and Australian yarns

The standard yarn categories produced in the United States, Australia and New Zealand differ slightly in weight from those common in Europe. A table of **approximate** American and Australian/New Zealand equivalents is given here. When you substitute one 'nationality' of yarn for another specificied in a pattern, buy just one ball to check that you can achieve successful results.

U.K.	U.S.	Australia/ New Zealand
2 and 3 ply	-	-
4 ply	Fingering	5 ply
DK	Sportweight	8 ply
Aran	Knitting worsted	12 ply
Chunky	Bulky	14 ply

TIP

Yarn unravelled from a newly knitted fabric can be wound into a ball while it is still attached to the knitting and re-used straightaway. If the yarn has been knitted up for some time and is very crinkly, cut it off, wind it up loosely and hold it over steam for a few minutes to ease out the crinkles, then re-wind it into a ball.

Holding the Yarn and Needles

HOLDING THE YARN AND NEEDLES

Before casting on stitches you must get to grips with the needles and yarn. At first they will seem awkward to hold but practice will soon make these manoeuvres familiar. Use a medium-weight yarn and a pair of medium-sized (4-5mm) needles to practise with. Ideally, get a friend who knits to cast on a few stitches for you, as it is easier to learn to handle the needles and yarn if some stitches are already on the needle.

Holding the yarn

In Britain and in other English-speaking countries, and in some European countries, the yarn is normally held in the right hand. In German-speaking countries and some other parts of the world, it is held in the left. The two methods are sometimes called the 'English' and 'Continental' methods, respectively. See which method you prefer. It is a good idea to learn both if you intend to do Fair Isle colour knitting, so as to be able to hold one colour in each hand.

There are various methods of winding the yarn around the fingers to control the tension of the yarn and so produce even knitting. In time you might develop a favourite way, but first try one of the methods shown here.

Method 1

Holding the yarn in the right or left hand, pass it under the little finger of the other hand, then around the same finger, over the third finger, under the middle finger and over the index finger. The index finger is used to pass the yarn around the needle tip, and having the yarn circled around the little finger creates the necessary tension for knitting evenly.

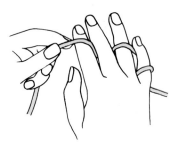

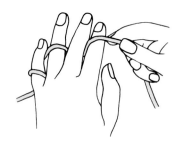

Method 2

Holding the yarn in the right or left hand, pass it under the little finger of the other hand, over the third finger, under the middle finger and over the index finger. The index finger is used

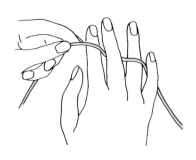

to pass the yarn around the needle tip, and tension is controlled by gripping the yarn in the crook of the little finger.

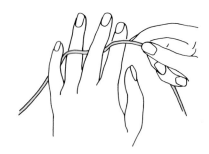

Holding the needles

The method of holding the needles depends on whether the yarn is held in the right or left hand.

Right-hand needle

For the English method, hold the right-hand needle as you would a pencil. For casting on and working the first few rows, the knitted piece passes between the thumb and the index finger. As the knitting grows, slide the thumb under

the knitted piece holding the needle from below.

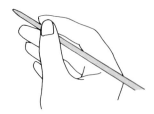

For the Continental method, hold the right-hand needle as shown below. The right thumb and fingers remain above the piece of knitting throughout the work.

Left-hand needle

This is held lightly over the top. If the English method of knitting (a) is preferred, use the thumb and index finger to control the tip. If the Continental method (b) is used, control the tip with the thumb and middle finger.

(a)

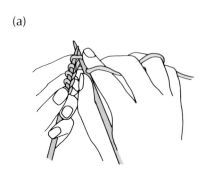

(b)

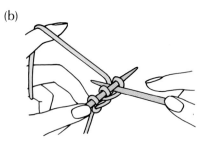

CASTING ON

'Casting on' is the term used for making a row of stitches to be used as a foundation for knitting. There are several methods of casting on which produce different kinds of edge. Some of the most useful of these are shown here and on pages 10 and 11. For your first attempts at knitting you may prefer to use just one method, but it is a good idea eventually to learn others as well for use in different situations.

Practise casting on until you can achieve a smooth, even edge.

Making a slip knot

A slip knot is the starting point for every piece of knitting.

Method 1

1. Loop the yarn as shown and slip the needle under the lower strand of the loop.

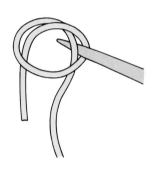

2. Holding the ends of the yarn with one hand, pull the needle upwards; this tightens the knot.

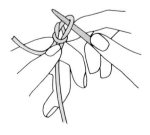

Method 2

1. Wind the yarn twice around the first two fingers of the left hand, then bend

the fingers so that the two loops are visible across the knuckles. Using a

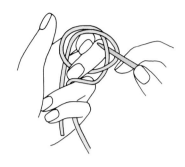

knitting needle in the right hand, pull the back thread through the front one to form a loop.

Continue following step 2 of method 1.

Finger and thumb method

This method requires only one needle. The right hand holds the needle, while the left holds the yarn. Once mastered, this technique is extremely quick and efficient and produces a very even cast-on edge. For a more elastic edge, hold two needles together in the right hand instead of one.

1. Allowing 2 cm [3/4 inch] per stitch, make a slip knot the required distance from the end of the yarn, on the needle held in the right hand.

2. Wind the cut end of the yarn around the left thumb from front to back. Wind the ball end of the yarn around the index finger of the left hand from front to back as shown. Hold both ends of the yarn in the palm of the left hand. * Insert the needle upwards through the yarn on the thumb, down through the front of the loop on the index finger, then back down through the front of the loop on the thumb.

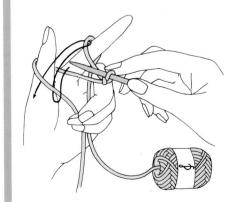

3. Pull the yarn through thus forming a loop on the needle.

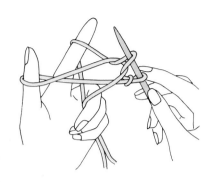

4. Remove the thumb from the loop, then re-insert it as shown, pulling downwards on the long cut yarn to tighten the loop on the needle.

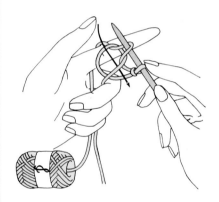

Move the thumb back to the original position. Repeat from the * until the required number of stitches has been cast on.

Left-handed knitters

Although the Continental and English methods of holding the yarn can both be used by right-handed people, if you are left-handed you may prefer to use the Continental method as it distributes the work more evenly between the two hands; in the English method almost all the work is done by the right hand.

Alternatively, you can simply **reverse** the English method, holding the yarn and the working needle in the left hand. To learn this method you will find it helpful to hold a mirror up to the illustrations.

Casting On

Thumb Method

This method of casting on, like the one on page 9, requires only one needle and produces the same elastic edge. It is more comfortable for knitters who hold the yarn in the right hand than for those who use the Continental method.

1. Make a slip knot the required length from the end of the yarn allowing about 2 cm (3/4 inch) per stitch. Hold the needle in the right hand with the ball end of yarn over your first finger. Hold the other end in the palm of your left hand. *Wind the loose end of the yarn around the left thumb from front to back.

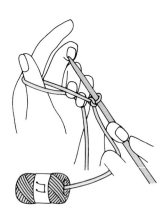

2. Insert the needle upwards through the yarn on the thumb.

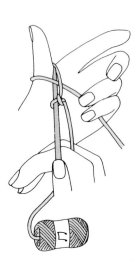

3. Loop the ball end of the yarn under, then over the point of the needle with your right index finger.

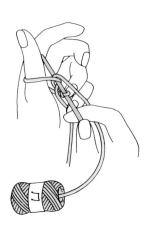

4. Draw the new loop back through the loop on the thumb to form a stitch.

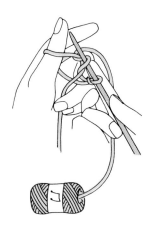

5. Slip your left thumb out of the first loop and pull the loose end to tighten the stitch. Repeat from the * until the required number of stitches has been cast on.

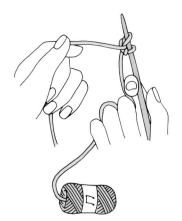

Cable Method

This method requires the use of two needles and gives a very firm, neat finish.

1. Make a slip knot near the cut end of the yarn on the left-hand needle.

2. Holding the yarn at the back of the needles, insert the right-hand needle upwards through the slip knot, and loop the yarn around the point of the right-hand needle.

3. Bring the right-hand needle and the new loop back through the slip knot so that you have a loop on each needle. Do not slip the original stitch off the left-hand needle.

4. Insert the left-hand needle from right to left through this loop and slip it off the right-hand needle. There are now two stitches on the left-hand needle.

5. Insert the right-hand needle between the two stitches on the left-hand needle. Loop the yarn around the point of the right-hand needle.

6. Draw the new loop through and place it on the left-hand needle as before.

Repeat steps 5 and 6 until the required number of stitches has been cast on.

BASIC STITCHES

The **knit** and **purl** stitches provide the basis of most knitted fabrics. The knit stitch is the easier to learn. Once you have mastered this, move on to the purl stitch, which is slightly more complicated.

Note: As each new stitch or technique is introduced, it will be followed by its abbreviation. The symbol used where pattern instructions are given in chart form is shown on page 24.

The knit stitch (k)

1. Hold the needle with the cast-on stitches in the left hand. With the yarn at the back of the work, insert the right-hand needle through the first stitch from front to back as shown.

2. Wind the yarn under and over the point of the right-hand needle.

3. Bring the right-hand needle and the new loop back through the first stitch on the left-hand needle.

4. Slip the original stitch off the left-hand needle.

To knit a row, repeat steps 1 to 4 until all the stitches have been transferred from the left needle to the right needle. Turn the work and transfer the needle holding the stitches to the left hand to work the next row.

Basic Fabrics

The purl stitch (p)

1. With the yarn at the front of the work, insert the right-hand needle through the first stitch from back to front as shown.

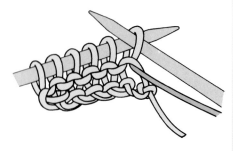

2. Loop the yarn over then under the point of the right-hand needle.

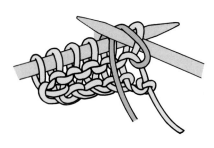

3. Take the right-hand needle and the new loop back through the first stitch.

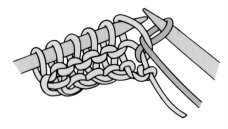

4. Slip the original stitch off the left-hand needle.

To purl a row, repeat steps 1 to 4 until all the stitches are transferred to the right-hand needle, then turn the work and transfer the needles to work the next row.

BASIC FABRICS

Using the two basic stitches - knit and purl - you can make some simple fabrics that occur frequently in knitting.

See photos and charted instructions on pages 26 and 27.

Garter stitch (g st)

This stitch is produced by knitting every row. This produces a reversible, relatively thick fabric with raised horizontal ridges on both sides of the work. One of the advantages of garter stitch is that it does not curl and so does not require an edging.

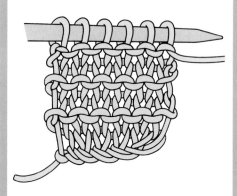

Stocking stitch (st st)

Stocking stitch is the most widely used knitted fabric. It consists of alternate knit and purl rows, with the knit side used as the right side. The fabric is flat and smooth. It tends to curl at the edges and so is normally finished with a band, border or hem.

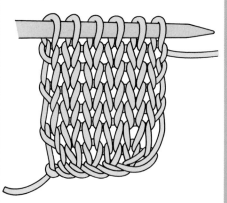

Reverse stocking stitch (rev st st)

This is the same as stocking stitch but with the ridged, purl, side of the fabric used as the right side. This fabric is often used as a background to cables, as it enhances their raised, smooth texture.

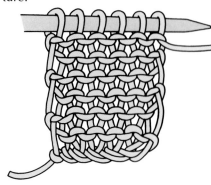

Single rib (k1 and p1)

This is formed by alternately knitting a stitch, then purling a stitch, to give unbroken vertical lines. It makes a very elastic fabric which is used mainly for borders such as welts, neckbands and cuffs. When used as an edging, rib is generally worked on smaller size needles than those used for the main fabric in order to ensure a snug fit.

1st row (right side):

1. Knit the first stitch.

2. Bring the yarn forward to the front of the work between the needles, and purl the next stitch.

3. Take the yarn to the back of the work between the needles, and knit the next stitch.

Repeat steps 2 and 3 until all stitches are transferred to the right-hand needle.

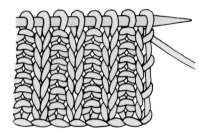

For an odd number of stitches this would be written as follows (see abbreviations page 24):

1st row (right side): K1, *p1, k1; rep from * to end.

2nd row: P1, *k1, p1; rep from * to end.

Rep these 2 rows.

Always ensure that stitches that are knitted on one row are purled on the following row, and vice versa. If an odd number of stitches is cast on, the right-side rows will always begin and end with a knit stitch while the wrong-side rows begin and end with a purl stitch. If an even number of stitches is cast on, every row will begin with a knit stitch and end with a purl stitch.

CASTING OFF

Once you have finished a piece of knitting, you must secure the stitches; this is called casting off. It is important that the cast-off edge have the same 'give' or elasticity as the rest of the fabric. Always cast off in the stitch used for the main fabric unless directed otherwise. If your cast-off edge tends to be tight, use a larger size needle.

Casting off knitwise

Knit the first two stitches. *Using the left-hand needle, lift the first stitch over the second and drop it off between the points of the two needles. Knit the next stitch; repeat from the * until all the stitches from the left-hand needle have been worked and only one stitch remains on the right-hand needle. Cut

the yarn (leaving enough to sew in the end) and thread the cut end through the stitch on the needle. Draw the yarn up firmly to fasten off the last stitch.

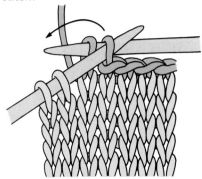

Casting off purlwise

Purl the first two stitches, then * using the left-hand needle, lift the first stitch over the second and drop it off the needle. Purl the next stitch; repeat from the * securing the last stitch as described above.

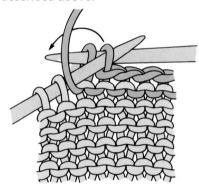

Casting off in rib

Always work the stitches as though you were working a row in rib, casting stitches off as you go. For example, for single rib, knit the first stitch, purl the second and cast off the first. Knit the next stitch and cast off the previous one. Continue in this way to the end. Rib should normally be cast off fairly loosely to keep the edge elastic.

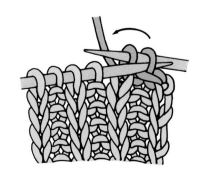

Correcting Mistakes

CORRECTING MISTAKES

Even the most experienced knitter makes the occasional mistake but there are very few mistakes that cannot subsequently be put right.

There are a few ways of avoiding making mistakes or seeing the error before you have worked too many rows above it. First, try out the stitch pattern in spare yarn before working the garment. In this way you will become familiar with the pattern and will be less likely to make a mistake. While working the garment, check back after every pattern row to make sure the pattern has been worked correctly. It is far easier and less frustrating to unravel one row than several. Some patterns involve increasing and decreasing stitches within the row. In such cases it is wise to count the stitches after each pattern row to make sure you have the correct number. If, despite these precautions, you still find you have made a mistake, don't despair; most mistakes can be remedied with a little patience.

Dropped stitches

This is a very common mistake. A stitch dropped on the row below the row in progress can be picked up and re-created on the needles. If the stitch has dropped down and formed a ladder, you can pick it up and re-work it. However, if you have continued knitting above the dropped stitch, the stitches above it will be drawn too tightly across the back of the work to leave enough spare yarn to re-create the lost stitches. In this case you should unravel the work down to the bottom of the ladder and re-knit the unravelled rows.

Picking up a knit stitch on the row below

Here, the next stitch on the left-hand needle has slipped off and pulled out of the stitch in the row below. Before a ladder can form it is possible to retrieve both of these stitches.

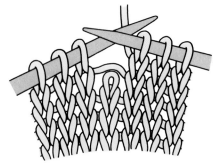

1. Insert the right-hand needle from front to back through the dropped stitch and under the horizontal strand from the row above, so that the strand lies **behind** the stitch.

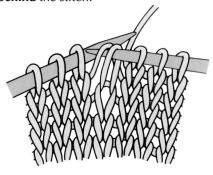

2. Insert the left-hand needle through the stitch from back to front and lift it over the strand and off the needle as though casting it off.

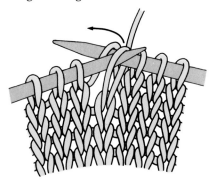

3. The stitch remaining on the right-hand needle must now be transferred back to the left-hand needle and turned so that it lies correctly.

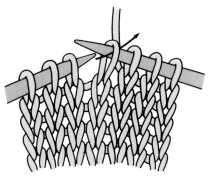

4. Insert the left-hand needle from front to back through this stitch turning it back into the correct position and slip it off the right-hand needle. It is now ready to be knitted.

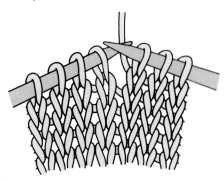

Picking up a purl stitch on the row below

This is the same situation as the previous one but on a purl row.

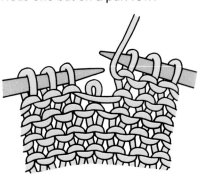

1. Take the yarn temporarily to the back and insert the right-hand needle from back to front through the dropped stitch and under the horizontal strand from the row above, so that the strand lies **in front of** the stitch.

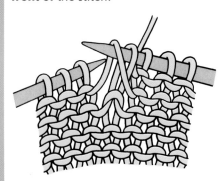

2. Take the left-hand needle behind the strand and slip it through the stitch as shown. Lift the point of the left-hand needle to open up the stitch a little.

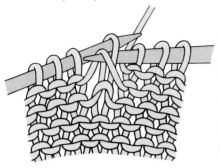

3. At the same time draw the right-hand needle and the strand back through this stitch.

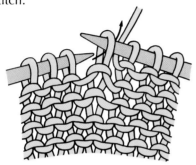

4. Insert the left-hand needle from front to back through the picked-up stitch and slip it off the right-hand needle. It is already lying in the correct position ready to be purled.

Re-working a ladder

If a dropped stitch is not noticed immediately it can easily form a ladder running down a number of rows. If possible, work from the knit side of the fabric. Insert a crochet hook into the free stitch with the hook pointing upwards, catch the first strand of the ladder from below and draw it forwards through the stitch. Continue up the ladder until all the strands have been worked, then replace the stitch on the left-hand needle, making sure that it lies correctly.

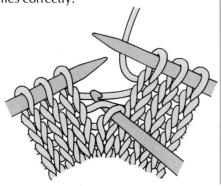

On some fabrics, such as garter stitch, you will need to pick up stitches on the purl side in a ladder. In this case, insert the hook from back to front, as shown, **over** the strand.

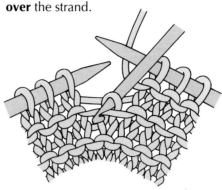

Unpicking

If the mistake is only one or two rows down, you can work back to it stitch by stitch. Keeping the needles and yarn in the normal working position, insert the left-hand needle from front to back through the centre of the first stitch **below** the stitch on the right-hand needle. Slip the right-hand needle out of the stitch above. Continue until you reach the stitch to be corrected.

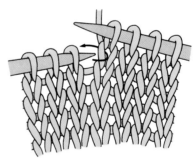

Unravelling

To go back stitch by stitch for several rows would be too tedious. The quick way is to take the work off the needle and unravel it. First, mark the row below the mistake. When you reach the row to be corrected, unpick it using a spare needle of a smaller size, thus preventing more dropped stitches as you try to get them back on to the needle. Unpick the stitches gently – do not tug on difficult stitches or they will become tighter. Jiggle the yarn so that the stitches ease themselves apart. You will need extra patience with textured or fluffy yarns. Use small nail scissors to cut away excess fibres taking care not to cut the yarn itself.

Simple Shaping

SIMPLE SHAPING

A knitted fabric can be shaped to make it narrower or wider by decreasing or increasing the number of stitches on the needle. The shaping can be worked at the end(s) of a row or within the row as, for example, when you need to work a 'mass increase' above ribbing to obtain extra fullness.

Decreasing one stitch

The simplest method of decreasing one stitch is to work two stitches together.

Knitting two together (K2tog)

Insert the right-hand needle from front to back through the **second** stitch on the left-hand needle and then through the first stitch, as shown, then knit them together as one stitch.

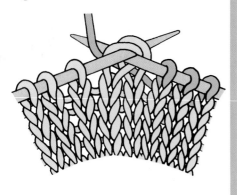

Purling two together (P2tog)

Insert the right-hand needle from back to front through the next two stitches, then purl them together as one stitch.

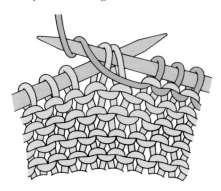

Increasing one stitch (inc 1)

The most usual method of increasing is to work twice into a stitch.

Knitwise increase

Work into the front and back of a stitch as follows: knit into the stitch, then without slipping it off the needle, twist the right-hand needle behind the left-hand one and knit again into the back of the loop, then slip the original stitch off the left-hand needle. There are now two stitches on the right-hand needle made from the original one.

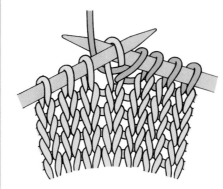

Purlwise increase

Purl into the front of the stitch as usual, then twist the needle around and purl into the back of it, then slip it off the needle.

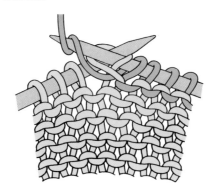

Making a stitch (M1K or M1P)

Another form of increasing involves working into the strand between two stitches.

1. Insert the right-hand needle from front to back under the strand lying between the stitches on the right- and left-hand needles.

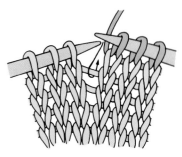

2. Lift the strand on to the left-hand needle. Insert the right-hand needle through the **back** of this newly formed loop and knit (or purl) into it. (By working into the back you twist the strand and so prevent the hole that would form if you were to work into the front of it).

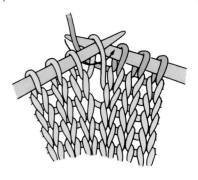

3. Slip the twisted strand off the left-hand needle. A new stitch has been formed between two existing stitches.

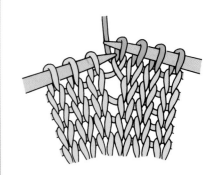

JOINING IN A NEW YARN

Always join in a new ball of yarn at the start of a row. If the fabric is smooth-textured it is easy to estimate whether there is enough yarn at the end of a ball to complete a row. Lay the knitting flat and see if the yarn reaches at least four times across the width. Allow an extra length or two for a heavily textured fabric. If you are sure you have enough for one row, but are unsure if it is enough for two, tie a loose knot half-way along the remaining length of yarn. Work one row; if you have not reached the knot there will be enough to work another row.

To make a perfect join at the edge of the work, simply drop the old yarn and start working the row with the new yarn. After a few stitches, tie the old and new ends in a loose knot. The ends can be darned into the seam at a later stage.

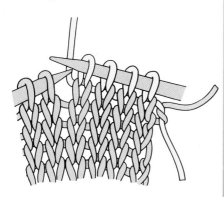

HORIZONTAL STRIPES

Once you have learned to work the basic fabrics shown on pages 12 and 13, you can easily add interest to them by working in horizontal stripe patterns. Horizontal stripes are achieved simply by changing colour at the end of certain rows. It is usually a good idea to work an even number of rows in each colour so that the colour change will always be at the same edge of the work (normally the right-hand edge) and you will not have to break off the yarn. You simply bring the new colour up in front of the old one and continue knitting with it.

If the stripes are not too deep (say no more than 5 cm [2 ins]) the yarn not in use can be carried **loosely** up the side of the work. If they are deeper, cross the yarns over at the edge on every alternate row to avoid tightening the

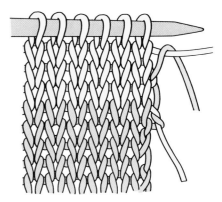

unused yarn. If they are very deep, or colour changes must be made at both sides of the work, you will need to join the old and new yarn.

By varying the basic horizontal stripe pattern, you can easily achieve a number of interesting effects. For example, changing colour produces neat, even lines on the knit side of stocking stitch but on the purl (reverse stocking stitch) side, you will find broken lines of colour where the changes occur which you might prefer to use as the right side of the work. An occasional purl row in a contrasting colour will give textural variation to the work.

TIPS

In knitting instructions you will often find the terms 'knitwise' and 'purlwise'. These mean, respectively, inserting the needle as you do to knit and as you do to purl.

* * * *

Occasionally, you will find a knot in a ball of yarn where it has broken during the manufacturing process and been re-joined. To avoid discovering one of these in mid-row and having to unpick stitches back to the beginning of the row, it is a good idea always to re-wind new yarn beginning a new ball where a knot appears.

Decorative Techniques

DECORATIVE TECHNIQUES

On these two pages we introduce two of the many decorative techniques that you can employ to bring interesting colour and textural effects into your knitting.

Slipping stitches

To slip a stitch is simply to move it from the left-hand to the right-hand needle without working into it. This technique can be used to create rich textures and multi-coloured effects, often called mosaic patterns.

To slip a stitch purlwise (sl 1 purlwise)

Insert the right-hand needle into the front of the next stitch on the left-hand needle from back to front, then slip the stitch off the left-hand needle.

Knit stitches, as well as purl stitches, should be slipped purlwise unless the pattern states otherwise, in order to keep the stitch aligned correctly.

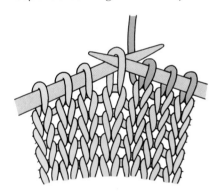

To slip a stitch knitwise (sl 1 knitwise)

Insert the right-hand needle into the front of the next stitch on the left-hand needle from front to back, then slip the stitch off the left-hand needle.

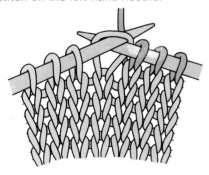

Keeping the yarn on the wrong side

When following a slip stitch pattern, unless otherwise instructed, carry the yarn across the wrong side of the work (the back of the work on right side rows, the front on wrong side rows).

The illustrations below show the wrong side of a fabric in which the row in progress is being knitted (to produce a purl ridge on the right side) and every alternate stitch slipped.

1. After the last stitch was knitted, the yarn was at the back (the right side). Before slipping the next stitch, bring the yarn forward between the needles.

2. Keeping the yarn in front, slip the next stitch, then take the yarn back between the needles, ready for knitting the next stitch.

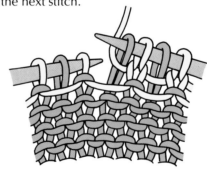

Yarn on the right side

Some slip stitch patterns break this rule to create interesting effects. If the yarn is held to the front on a right side row while stitches are slipped, or to the back on a wrong side row, this produces a 'bar' across the slipped stitch(es).

If the yarn is to be held on the right side, the instructions will specify this usually with an abbreviation such as 'yf' (on a right-side row) or 'yb' (on a wrong-side row).

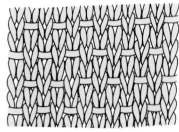

slip stitch 'bar'

Mosaic patterns

Mosaic patterns give the impression that two or more colours have been used in the same row. In reality, only one colour is used at a time and colours are changed as for horizontal stripes (see page 17). Multi-coloured effects are achieved by slipping stitches of one colour over rows of stitches worked in another colour.

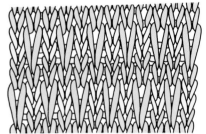

mosaic effect

Basic cables

Cables are often associated with traditional Aran patterns in which they represent the ropes used by the fishermen of the Aran Isles. However, they are also used with all sorts of other patterns, including lace, and colour to achieve beautiful effects.

Cabling is simply a method of moving a group of stitches across another. One set of stitches is held at the back or front on a short cable needle, while the following group is knitted; then the held stitches are knitted, thus producing a twisted effect, either to the right or to the left. The number of stitches contained in a rope cable varies, but four, six and eight are the most common. In the patterns on page 19 only four stitches are cabled; larger numbers are slightly more awkward to handle.

Cabling is normally worked on a right side row.

Decorative Techniques

Cable four back (C4B)

Here the cable consists of four stitches in stocking stitch against a reverse stocking stitch background; this is the most usual arrangement - the purled fabric setting off the smooth knit texture of the coils.

1. On a right side row, work to the position of the cable and slip the next two stitches on to the cable needle.

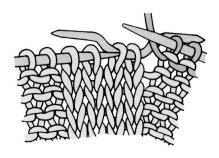

2. Hold the stitches on the cable needle at the **back** of the work, then knit the next two stitches from the left-hand needle.

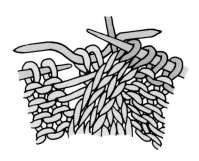

3. Now knit the two stitches from the cable needle. This produces a cable that twists to the right.

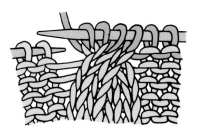

Cable four front (C4F)

1. Work to the position of the cable, then slip the next two stitches on to the cable needle; leave the cable needle at the **front** of the work.

2. Working behind the cable needle, knit the next two stitches from the left-hand needle.

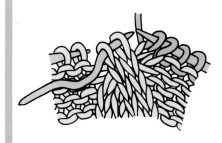

3. Now knit the two stitches from the cable needle. This produces a cable that twists to the left.

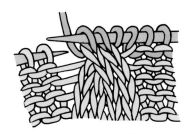

Working from a Pattern

WORKING FROM A PATTERN

Before starting to knit any pattern, always read it through. This will give you an idea of how the garment is structured and the techniques involved. The styles of writing and presentation vary according to the publisher but each pattern includes the following elements.

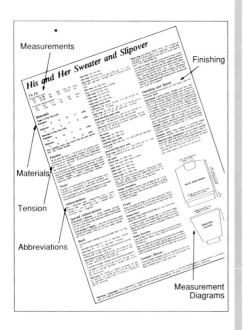

Measurements/sizes

Most knitting patterns give instructions for a range of chest or bust sizes. You should normally work to your actual body measurement as the designer will have decided how much 'ease' should be included in the design, and will have calculated the instructions accordingly. However, if the garment illustrated appears too baggy for your taste, knit a smaller size; make a larger size if you prefer garments with a lot of room.

Most patterns give a 'finished measurement' for each of the various sizes, so you will know how much ease has been allowed. Some patterns also have measurement diagrams which give the shape and measurements of each pattern piece. Patterns given in a range of sizes have instructions for the smallest size printed first, followed by the other sizes in brackets or parentheses. For example, 'Cast on 26(28-30-32) sts'.

This instruction gives information for 4 sizes at the same time. To avoid confusion, go through the pattern beforehand and underline or circle all the instructions for the size you are making. Take special care if the sizes have been separated for a particular instructions. For example, suppose the pattern states '**1st (4th) sizes only:** Cast off 15(20) sts, work to end.' For the 1st size, follow the instructions outside the ( )s, and for the 4th size follow those within them. For any other size, these instructions do not apply.

Materials

This heading gives a list of all the materials required for making the garment, including amount of yarn (according to size), needles and buttons.

Tension/gauge

Tension is a vitally important part of the pattern and one that many knitters overlook. This figure determines the finished measurements of the garment. If you wish the garment to be the correct size, you **must** obtain the same number of stitches per centimetre/inch as the designer did. Even a small difference in tension can produce a considerable difference across the width of a garment.

The tension/gauge is normally given over a measurement of 10 cm [4 ins], for example: '25 sts and 30 rows = 10 cm [4 ins] square measured over st st using 4mm needles'.

To check the tension, cast on a few more stitches than the number given and, using the specified needles, work a few more rows than given. Cast off. Lay the swatch on a flat, padded surface (some yarns may need blocking or pressing; see page 22). Count off the specified number of stitches and insert a pin to either side. Place a ruler or tape measure on the work and measure the distance between the pins. It should be 10 cm [4 ins] (or the measurement given). If it is greater, your tension is looser than the pattern designer's; change to smaller needles and make another swatch. If the measurement is

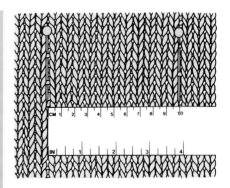

smaller change to larger needles. Repeat, if necessary, until the tension is correct. Use the needles that produce the correct tension for knitting the garment and adjust the other needle sizes (e.g. those for the ribbing) to correspond.

Similarly, count the number of rows (this is more easily done on the ridged, purl side of stocking stitch).

Row tension is not quite so important when length measurements are given. However, it is important where the instructions are given in rows and it is necessary to work to a certain position within a pattern repeat before commencing armhole, neck or shoulder shaping. And it is obviously important in a garment that is knitted sideways, where it becomes the horizontal measurement.

If the tension is given over a stitch pattern other than stocking stitch, you will need to count the stitches in the pattern repeat (see page 21) and cast on a multiple of that number exceeding the number given in the tension. In some complex patterns you should mark off this number on one row with two contrasting loops of yarn to avoid having to count the stitches later.

Abbreviations

Knitting instructions are normally given in an abbreviated form which saves valuable space. A pattern leaflet will include a list of the abbreviations used for that pattern. Booklets may give a single list of basic abbreviations for all the patterns, plus any special abbreviations along with the pattern to which they apply.

The abbreviations used in this book are given on page 24.

Working from a Pattern

Garment instructions

Actual working instructions are written in such a way that they should be self-explanatory. If metric and imperial/standard measurements are given, always work either in one system or the other; **do not** mix the two.

Asterisks, brackets or parentheses are used to indicate the repetition of a sequence of stitches. For example: '*K3, p1; rep from * to end.' This means knit three stitches, then purl one stitch alternately to the end of the row. It could also be written: '[K3, p1] to end'.

Asterisks and brackets or parentheses may be used together in a row: '*K4, p1, [k1, p1] 3 times; rep from * to end'. Part of the instruction is placed in brackets to indicate that these stitches only are to be repeated three times before returning to the instructions immediately after the asterisk.

When repeating anything, make sure that you are doing so for the correct number of times. For example: '[K1, p1] twice' = 4 stitches worked, but '*K1, p1; rep from * twice more' = 6 stitches worked in all.

You may come across the phrase 'work straight' or 'work even'. This means continue without increasing or decreasing the number of stitches on the needle, keeping the pattern correct as established.

If you encounter the figure 0 within an instruction, for example 'K1(0-1-2)', this means that for **that particular size** no stitches are worked at that point.

When you put your knitting aside, always mark where you are on the pattern. You may think that you will remember but it is better to be safe than sorry, especially if a complex stitch is involved.

Pattern repeats or multiples

Most stitch patterns, apart from the most basic fabrics, consist of a set of stitches that are repeated across the row and a number of rows that are repeated throughout the length of the fabric. If a pattern is symmetrical (a diamond pattern for example), it is important that each row begin and end in the same way to 'balance' the row. In other words, if a pattern begins 'K3, p1, k5' the row should end 'k5, p1, k3'. This ensures that when seams are joined the pattern is symmetrical on either side of the seam. This rule does not apply to non-symmetrical patterns such as diagonal patterns, which cannot begin and end in the same way.

A pattern repeat within knitting instructions either is contained within brackets or parentheses or follows an asterisk. The extra stitches outside the brackets or before the asterisk are the stitches required to balance the pattern. Sometimes extra stitches are given to make the written instructions clearer to follow. To work out the number of stitches in a pattern repeat, simply add together the stitches within the brackets or after the asterisk (i.e. the stitches that are to be repeated).

Finishing or making up

This part of the pattern will tell you whether to block or press the work and how to join the various sections. Often it will include instructions for picking up stitches (see page 22) for a neckband or collar, for example. Always follow the sequence recommended in the pattern. Sometimes various processes (such as embroidery) are easier to work at a certain stage, and sections fit together more logically than would appear at first glance.

Stitch Pattern Multiples

The multiple or repeat of each stitch pattern plus the number of stitches needed to 'balance' the row is given with the written instructions.

To make working from the written instructions easier, in some instances one extra repeat has been added to the balancing stitches; THESE EXTRA STITCHES ARE NOT NEEDED ON THE CHARTS.

For example: Moss Rib on page 28.

Multiple of 4 sts + 5.

1st row (right side): K2, *p1, k3; rep from * to last 3 sts, p1, k2.

2nd row: P1, *k3, p1; rep from * to end.

Rep these 2 rows.

The chart shows the 4 repeat stitches and 1 balancing stitch (5 sts).

The written instructions include one extra repeat (multiple of 4 sts + 4 + 1 balancing stitch) therefore a minimum of 9 stitches must be worked.

Rep these 4 sts

Picking Up Stitches

PICKING UP STITCHES

Once the main body of the knitting is complete, it is often necessary to pick up stitches along one or more edges to work a band or collar. The technique used is normally referred to as 'pick up and knit' or 'knit up'.

These new stitches are then worked in the appropriate stitch – usually ribbing. Care must be taken to ensure that the stitches are divided evenly along the length of the fabric and also that they are picked up through **either** a whole stitch **or** half a stitch throughout to produce a clean, unbroken line along the edge. To pick up the stitches, use a needle one or two sizes smaller than those used for the main fabric.

If the stitches are picked up across a row of stitches (cast-on or cast-off edges) they can be picked up stitch for stitch, if the number to be picked up is the same. If they are picked up along a vertical or shaped edge, you will probably find that not every stitch or row needs to be worked into.

To calculate how to pick the stitches up evenly, lay the edge to be used straight and measure the length. Place a pin at the halfway point at right angles to the edge, then halve these distances again and again to get eight equal sections. Divide the given number of stitches by eight, and pick up approximately this number in each section, checking that the total number of stitches has been picked up at the end. Always work into the first and last stitches at either end to prevent a gap.

Working along a cast-on/cast-off edge

With the right side of the work facing you, insert the needle from front to back under **both** loops of the first stitch, wind the yarn around the needle as if to knit

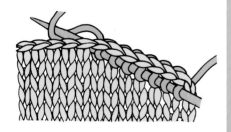

and draw a loop through. Continue in this way for as many stitches as are required.

Working along a side edge

Work as for a cast-on or cast-off edge but inserting the needle between the first and second stitch of the first row (that is, one whole stitch in from the edge) and continuing along the edge, missing a row occasionally as required, to obtain the correct number of stitches. If the yarn is very thick, work through the centre of the edge stitch, thus taking in only half a stitch and reducing the bulk.

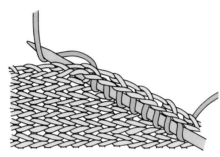

Working along an edge with held stitches

Some edges, such as for a crew neckline, involve a combination of working across stitches previously left on a holder – say at the centre front neck – and picking up stitches. When you reach the stitches on a holder, slip them on to another needle, then **knit** across them.

BLOCKING AND PRESSING

Before the individual pieces of knitting can be joined they must normally be blocked and, in some cases, pressed. These processes smooth out irregularities and help the sections to fit together correctly.

Blocking

To block a piece of knitting you will need a flat, padded surface covered with a clean cloth and some long dressmaker's pins.

1. Place the piece of knitting on the padded surface, wrong side up if the fabric is flat and will be pressed later;

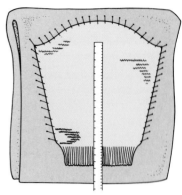

otherwise right side up. Place pins at frequent (2 cm [1 inch]) intervals and angle them through the very edge of the knitting into the padding avoiding any ribbed sections.

2. Check that the measurements are correct and that the lines of stitches are straight, both horizontally and vertically. Re-pin as necessary to achieve the correct size and shape, stretching or easing in slightly if required, so that the outline forms a smooth edge between the pins.

3. If the yarn should not be pressed, or if the pattern has a texture that would be spoiled by pressing, spray the work with water from a plant-misting bottle, or place a wet tea towel over it. Leave the knitting to dry.

Pressing

Pattern instructions will usually state whether the work should be pressed and, if so, how. If they do not, check the ball band. This will usually give the setting of the iron and state whether or not steam can be used. If in doubt, try pressing the tension swatch. Use a light touch; do not let the full weight of the iron rest on the knitting. A pressing cloth – dry for a steam iron, damp for a dry iron – helps to protect the fabric.

JOINING THE SEAMS

There are several different ways of sewing up a knitted garment. Two of the most commonly used are the backstitch and the flat seam.

Backstitch seam

This seam is strong and suitable for side, sleeve and shoulder seams but it must be worked carefully to prevent a bulky effect. Work no more that one stitch in from the edge; if a chunky yarn has been used for the garment, use a matching finer yarn for the stitching.

1. Pin the pieces together with right sides facing, matching pattern for pattern and row for row, and thread a large tapestry needle with yarn.

Anchor the yarn with a couple of stitches on the very edge, then take it around both edges of the fabric twice, thus enclosing them with a strong double stitch, ending with the yarn on the side facing you.

2. Insert the needle into the work just behind where the yarn emerges and bring it up one knitted stitch ahead.

3. Take the needle down where the previous stitch ended and bring it up ahead of the next knitted stitch to make a stitch twice as long on the wrong side as on the right.

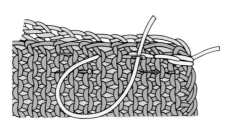

Repeat step 3 to make a continuous line of stitches of equal length on the side of the work facing you. On the reverse side the stitches form a straight, but slightly overlapping line. Do not pull the stitches too tightly. Check after every few stitches that the seam is not too tight in relation to the knitted fabric.

If the yarn may be pressed, open the seam and press it carefully with the **point** of the iron.

Flat seam

A flat seam is a method of **oversewing** or **overcasting** which, when opened out, is completely flat. It can be used for joining ribbed sections of a garment such as welts and cuffs, and for attaching button bands and collars where flatness and neatness are essential.

1. Lay the two pieces together with right sides facing, matching the edges exactly. Pin the work a few stitches in from the edge to allow room for your left index finger between the two fabrics.

2. Insert a threaded tapestry needle from back to front through the two thicknesses as close to the edge as possible. Pull the yarn through and repeat this action, making two or three stitches in the same place to secure the yarn at the beginning of the seam. Take short stitches through both thicknesses as shown, close to the edge.

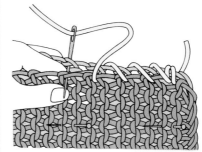

Abbreviations and Symbols

HOW TO READ CHARTS

Charts are read exactly as the knitting is worked from the bottom to the top. After the last row at the top has been worked, repeat the sequence from row 1. Each symbol represents an instruction. Symbols have been designed to resemble the actual appearance of the knitting.

Before starting to knit, look up all the symbols on your chosen chart so that you are familiar with the techniques involved. **Make sure you understand the difference between working similar symbols on a right side row and a wrong side row.**

Each square represents a stitch and each horizontal line a row. Place a ruler above the line you are working. If you are new to chart reading try comparing the charted instructions with the written ones.

Coloured patterns include suggested colours, indicated by a letter at the beginning of each row.

Right Side and Wrong Side Rows

A 'right side row' is one in which the right side is facing you as you work and a 'wrong side row' is one in which the wrong side is facing as you work. Row numbers are shown at the side of the charts **at the beginning of the row.** Right side rows are always read from right to left. Wrong side rows are always read from left to right.

Symbols on the charts are shown as they appear from the right side of the work. Therefore, a horizontal dash stands for a purl 'bump' on the right side regardless of whether it was achieved by purling on a right side row or knitting on a wrong side row. To make things clearer, symbols on right side rows are slightly darker than on wrong side rows.

Pattern Repeats and Multiples

In charted instructions the pattern repeat is contained between heavier vertical lines. The extra stitches not included in the pattern repeat are there to 'balance' the row or make it symmetrical and are worked only once.

Panels

Panels are patterns worked over a given number of stitches without necessarily being repeated.

All the panels in this book have been worked on a suggested background stitch. On the charts this is indicated by two stitches at either side of the panel. To work any of the panels you must cast on enough stitches to work the panel plus the required number of background stitches on each side.

Abbreviations and Symbols

The following abbreviations and symbols include all those used in this book.

Alt = alternate; **beg** = beginning; **cm** = centimetre(s); **dec** = decrease; **inc** = increase; **ins** = inches; **k** = knit; **m** = metres; **mm** = millimetre(s); **p** = purl; **psso** = pass slipped stitch over; **rep** = repeat; **sl** = slip; **st(s)** = stitch(es); **st st** = stocking stitch (1 row knit, 1 row purl); **tog** = together; **yb** = yarn back; **yf** = yarn forward.

Inc 1 (Inc 1K or Inc 1P) = Increase 1 st knitwise or purlwise by knitting or purling into front and back of next st.

M1 (M1K or M1P) = Make 1 st knitwise or purlwise by picking up strand of yarn lying between last st worked and next st and knitting or purling into back of it.

| I | **K** knit on right side rows

| − | **K** knit on wrong side rows

| − | **P** purl on right side rows

| I | **P** purl on wrong side rows

| S | **sl 1** slip one st purlwise with yarn at back of work, on right side rows.

| S | **sl 1** slip one st purlwise with yarn at front of work, on wrong side rows.

| S | **sl 1** slip one st purlwise with yarn at front of work, on right side rows.

| S | **sl 1** slip one st purlwise with yarn at back of work, on wrong side rows.

C4B (Cable 4 Back) slip next 2 sts on to cable needle and hold at back of work, knit next 2 sts from left-hand needle, then knit sts from cable needle (on right side rows).

C4F (Cable 4 Front) slip next 2 sts on to cable needle and hold at front of work, knit next 2 sts from left-hand needle, then knit sts from cable needle (on right side rows).

Note: Symbols are dark on right side rows and light on wrong side rows.

Sample Chart

1 stitch
1 row
wrong side rows start this side
right side rows start this side
tint indicates instruction involving more than 1 stitch
Rep these 12 sts
pattern repeat
stitches to balance pattern

Note: For meaning of each symbol refer to abbreviations.

KNITTING starting STITCHES

2

Easy does it ...
Try these simple knit and purl
textures and make a warm scarf
or a trio of scatter cushions.

Basic Fabrics

Stocking Stitch

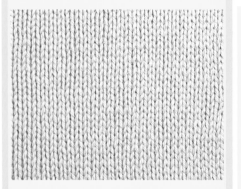

Any number of stitches.

1st row (right side): Knit every stitch.

2nd row: Purl every stitch.

Rep these 2 rows.

Any number of stitches

Stocking Stitch Stripes

Any number of stitches.

1st row (right side): Using A knit.

2nd row: Using A purl.

3rd and 4th rows: Rep these 2 rows once more.

5th row: Using B knit.

6th row: Using B purl.

7th and 8th rows: Rep the last 2 rows once more.

9th row: Using C knit.

10th row: Using C purl.

11th and 12th rows: Rep the last 2 rows once more.

Rep these 12 rows.

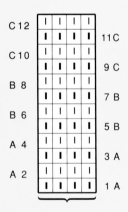

Any number of stitches

Garter Stitch

Any number of stitches.

1st row (right side): Knit every stitch.

2nd row: Knit every stitch.

Rep these 2 rows.

Any number of stitches

Reverse Stocking Stitch

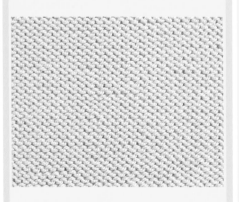

Work as given for stocking stitch, using purl side as right side.

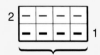

Any number of stitches

2 and 2 Rib

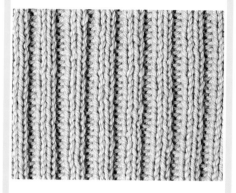

Multiple of 4 sts + 2.

1st row (right side): K2, *p2, k2; rep from * to end.

2nd row: P2, *k2, p2; rep from * to end.

Rep these 2 rows.

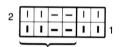

Rep these 4 sts

Garter Stitch Ridges

Any number of stitches.

1st row (right side): Knit.

2nd row: Purl.

3rd and 4th rows: Rep these 2 rows once more.

5th to 10th rows: Purl every row.

Rep these 10 rows.

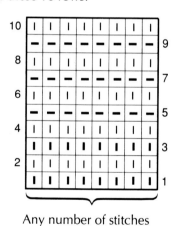

Any number of stitches

Single Rib (1 and 1)

Multiple of 2 sts + 1.

1st row (right side): K1, *p1, k1; rep from * to end.

2nd row: P1, *k1, p1; rep from * to end.

Rep these 2 rows.

Rep these 2 sts

2 and 1 Rib

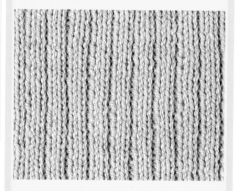

Multiple of 3 sts + 2.

1st row (right side): K2, *p1, k2; rep from * to end.

2nd row: P2, *k1, p2; rep from * to end.

Rep these 2 rows.

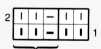

Rep these 3 sts

For Step by Step instructions for working Single Rib refer to page 12.

Simple Textures

Moss Stitch I

Multiple of 2 + 1.

1st row (right side): K1, *p1, k1; rep from * to end.

2nd row: K1, *p1, k1; rep from * to end.

Rep these 2 rows.

Rep these 2 sts

Moss Stitch II

Work as given for Moss Stitch I **but** working 2 rows in colour A, 2 rows in B, 2 rows in A and 2 rows in C throughout.

Double Moss Stitch

Multiple of 2 sts + 1.

1st row (right side): K1, *p1, k1; rep from * to end.

2nd row: P1, *k1, p1; rep from * to end.

3rd row: P1, *k1, p1; rep from * to end.

4th row: K1, *p1, k1; rep from * to end.

Rep these 4 rows.

Rep these 2 sts

Broken Rib

Multiple of 2 sts + 1.

1st row (right side): Knit.

2nd row: P1, *k1, p1; rep from * to end.

Rep these 2 rows.

Rep these 2 sts

Moss Rib

Multiple of 4 sts + 5.

1st row (right side): K2, *p1, k3; rep from * to last 3 sts, p1, k2.

2nd row: P1, *k3, p1; rep from * to end.

Rep these 2 rows.

Rep these 4 sts

Ridged Rib

Multiple of 2 sts + 1.

1st row (right side): Knit.

2nd row: Knit.

3rd row: P1, *k1, p1; rep from * to end.

4th row: K1, *p1, k1; rep from * to end.

Rep these 4 rows.

Rep these 2 sts

Seed Stitch I

Multiple of 4 sts + 3.

1st row (right side): P1, k1, *p3, k1; rep from * to last st, p1.

2nd row: K3, *p1, k3; rep from * to end.

Rep these 2 rows.

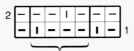

Rep these 4 sts

Seed Stitch II

Work as given for Seed Stitch I, using reverse side as right side.

Uneven Rib

Multiple of 4 sts + 3.

1st row (right side): *K2, p2; rep from * to last 3 sts, k2, p1.

2nd row: *K2, p2; rep from * to last 3 sts, k2, p1.

Rep these 2 rows.

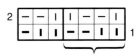

Rep these 4 sts

Fleck Stitch

Multiple of 2 sts + 1.

1st row (right side): Knit.

2nd row: Purl.

3rd row: K1, *p1, k1; rep from * to end.

4th row: Purl.

Rep these 4 rows.

Rep these 2 sts

Scarf

Measurements

Width 24 cm [9½ ins]
Length 125 cm [49 ins] excluding fringe.

Materials

Chunky knitting yarn

250 grams (9 ounces).

Pair needles size 6mm (UK 4, USA 10).

The quantities of yarn stated are based on average requirements and are therefore approximate.

For abbreviations see page 24.

Tension

15 sts and 20 rows = 10 cm [4 ins] square measured over st st.

Cast on 44 sts and commence rib pattern.

1st row (right side): K4, *p4, k4; rep from * to end.

2nd row: P4, *k4, p4; rep from * to end.

These 2 rows form the rib pattern. Rep these 2 rows until Scarf measures 125 cm [49 ins]. Cast off in pattern.

To Finish

Do not press. Attach fringe to each end if required.

Fringe

*Cut 5 lengths of yarn each 20 cm [8 ins] long. Fold in half and draw loop through first st at one end of Scarf. Draw ends of yarn through loop and tighten, thus forming a tassel. Rep from * along each end of Scarf at 1 cm [½ inch] intervals. Trim ends of fringe.

All-over Textures

Beaded Rib

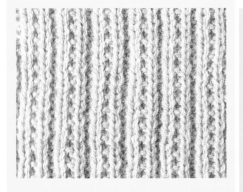

Multiple of 5 sts + 2.

1st row (right side): P2, *k1, p1, k1, p2; rep from * to end.

2nd row: K2, *p3, k2; rep from * to end.

Rep these 2 rows.

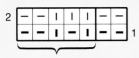

Rep these 5 sts

Woven Stitch

Multiple of 4 sts + 2.

1st row (right side): Knit.

2nd row: Purl.

3rd row: K2, *p2, k2; rep from * to end.

4th row: P2, *k2, p2; rep from * to end.

5th and 6th rows: As 1st and 2nd rows.

7th row: P2, *k2, p2; rep from * to end.

8th row: K2, *p2, k2; rep from * to end.

Rep these 8 rows.

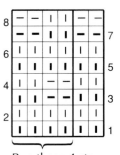

Rep these 4 sts

Check Pattern

Multiple of 3 sts + 1.

1st row (right side): Knit.

2nd row: Purl.

3rd row: K1, *p2, k1; rep from * to end.

4th row: Purl.

Rep these 4 rows.

Rep these 3 sts

Banded Rib

Multiple of 2 sts + 1.

1st row (right side): K1, *p1, k1; rep from * to end.

2nd row: P1, *k1, p1; rep from * to end.

3rd to 6th rows: Rep these 2 rows twice more.

7th row: P1, *k1, p1; rep from * to end.

8th row: K1, *p1, k1; rep from * to end.

9th to 12th rows: Rep the last 2 rows twice more.

Rep these 12 rows.

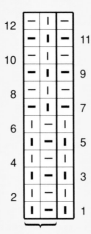

Rep these 2 sts

Double Fleck Stitch

Multiple of 6 sts + 4.

1st row (right side): Knit.

2nd row: P4, *k2, p4; rep from * to end.

3rd row: Knit.

4th row: P1, k2, *p4, k2; rep from * to last st, p1.

Rep these 4 rows.

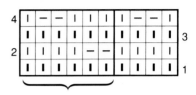

Rep these 6 sts

Oblique Rib

Multiple of 4 sts + 4.

1st row (right side): *K2, p2; rep from * to end.

2nd row: K1, *p2, k2; rep from * to last 3 sts, p2, k1.

3rd row: *P2, k2; rep from * to end.

4th row: P1, *k2, p2; rep from * to last 3 sts, k2, p1.

Rep these 4 rows.

Rep these 4 sts

Diagonal Stitch

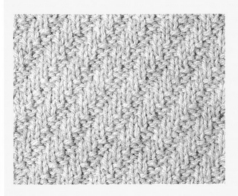

Multiple of 4 sts + 4.

1st row (right side): *K2, p2; rep from * to end.

2nd row: *K2, p2; rep from * to end.

3rd row: K1, *p2, k2; rep from * to last 3 sts, p2, k1.

4th row: P1, *k2, p2; rep from * to last 3 sts, k2, p1.

5th row: *P2, k2; rep from * to end.

6th row: *P2, k2; rep from to end.

7th row: P1, *k2, p2; rep from * to last 3 sts, k2, p1.

8th row: K1, *p2, k2; rep from * to last 3 sts, p2, k1.

Rep these 8 rows.

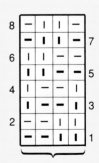

Rep these 4 sts

All-over Textures

Piqué Triangles

Multiple of 5 sts.

1st row (right side): *P1, k4; rep from * to end.

2nd row: *P3, k2; rep from * to end.

3rd row: *P3, k2; rep from * to end.

4th row: *P1, k4; rep from * to end.

Rep these 4 rows.

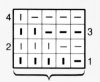

Rep these 5 sts

Double Ridged Rib

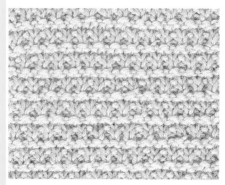

Multiple of 2 sts + 1.

1st row (right side): Knit.

2nd row: Knit.

3rd row: P1, *k1, p1; rep from * to end.

4th row: K1, *p1, k1; rep from * to end.

5th and 6th rows: As 1st and 2nd rows.

7th row: K1, *p1, k1; rep from * to end.

8th row: P1, *k1, p1; rep from * to end.

Rep these 8 rows.

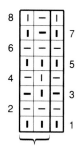

Rep these 2 sts

Diamond Panels

Multiple of 8 sts + 9 .

1st row (right side): Knit.

2nd row: K1, *p7, k1; rep from * to end.

3rd row: K4, *p1, k7; rep from * to last 5 sts, p1, k4.

4th row: K1, *p2, k1, p1, k1, p2, k1; rep from * to end.

5th row: K2, *[p1, k1] twice, p1, k3; rep from * to last 7 sts, [p1, k1] twice, p1, k2.

6th row: As 4th row.

7th row: As 3rd row.

8th row: As 2nd row.

Rep these 8 rows.

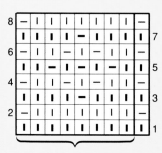

Rep these 8 sts

Simple Seed Stitch

Multiple of 4 sts + 5.

1st row (right side): P1, *k3, p1; rep from * to end.

2nd row: Purl.

3rd row: Knit.

4th row: Purl.

5th row: K2, p1, *k3, p1; rep from * to last 2 sts, k2.

6th to 8th rows: As 2nd to 4th rows.

Rep these 8 rows.

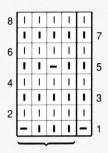

Rep these 4 sts

Diagonal Garter Ribs

Multiple of 5 sts + 2.

1st and every alt row (right side): Knit.

2nd row: *P2, k3; rep from * to last 2 sts, p2.

4th row: K1, *p2, k3; rep from * to last st, p1.

6th row: K2, *p2, k3; rep from * to end.

8th row: *K3, p2; rep from * to last 2 sts, k2.

10th row: P1, *k3, p2; rep from * to last st, k1.

Rep these 10 rows.

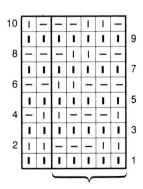

Rep these 5 sts

Knife Pleats

Multiple of 13 sts.

1st row (right side): *K4, [p1, k1] 3 times, p3; rep from * to end.

2nd row: *K3, [p1, k1] 3 times, p4; rep from * to end.

Rep these 2 rows.

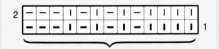

Rep these 13 sts

Measurements

Finished Cushions measure approximately 40 x 40 cm [16 x 16 ins].

Materials

Aran knitting yarn

Check Pattern Cushion

	250	grams
	9	ounces

Striped Cushion

Colour A	200	grams
	7	ounces
Colour B	50	grams
	2	ounces

Square Pattern Cushion

	300	grams
	11	ounces

Pair needles size 4½ mm (UK 7, USA 7).

Cushion pad 40 cm [16 ins] square. 40 cm [16 inch] zip.

The quantities of yarn stated are based on average requirements and are therefore approximate.

For abbreviations see page 24.

Tension

19 sts and 25 rows = 10 cm [4 ins] square measured over st st.

Check Pattern Cushion

Back and Front (Alike)

Cast on 75 sts and commence pattern.

1st row (right side): K3, *p3, k3; rep from * to end.

2nd row: P3, *k3, p3; rep from * to end.

3rd and 4th rows: Rep these 2 rows once more.

5th row: P3, *k3, p3; rep from * to end.

6th row: K3, *p3, k3; rep from * to end.

7th and 8th rows: Rep the last 2 rows once more.

These 8 rows form the pattern. Continue in pattern until Cushion measures 40 cm [16 ins] ending with a wrong side row. Cast off in pattern.

Striped Cushion

Back and Front (Alike)

Using A, cast on 76 sts and commence pattern.

1st row (right side): Using A, knit.

2nd row: Using A, purl.

3rd to 8th rows: Rep these 2 rows 3 times more.

9th row: Using B, knit.

10th row: Using B, knit.

These 10 rows form the pattern. Continue in pattern until Cushion measures approximately 40 cm [16 ins] ending with an 8th row of pattern. Cast off in pattern.

Square Pattern Cushion

Back and Front (Alike)

Cast on 75 sts and commence pattern.

1st row (right side): K1, *p1, k1; rep from * to end.

2nd row: K1, *p1, k1; rep from * to end.

3rd row: [K1, p1] twice, *k7, p1, k1, p1; rep from * to last st, k1.

4th row: K1, p1, k1, *p9, k1; rep from * to last 2 sts, p1, k1.

5th to 10th rows: Rep the last 2 rows 3 times more.

These 10 rows form the pattern. Continue in pattern until Cushion measures approximately 40 cm [16 ins] ending with a 2nd row. Cast off in pattern.

To Finish all Cushions

Press according to instructions on page 22 if required. Machine or hand stitch the cast on edge of both squares to each side of the zip. Join the 3 remaining sides of Cushion and insert cushion pad.

All-over Textures

Double Parallelogram Stitch

Multiple of 10 sts + 10.

1st row (right side): *P5, k5; rep from * to end.

2nd row: K1, *p5, k5; rep from * to last 9 sts, p5, k4.

3rd row: P3, *k5, p5; rep from * to last 7 sts, k5, p2.

4th row: K3, *p5, k5; rep from * to last 7 sts, p5, k2.

5th row: P1, *k5, p5; rep from * to last 9 sts, k5, p4.

6th row: P4, *k5, p5; rep from * to last 6 sts, k5, p1.

7th row: K2, *p5, k5; rep from * to last 8 sts, p5, k3.

8th row: P2, *k5, p5; rep from * to last 8 sts, k5, p3.

9th row: K4, *p5, k5; rep from * to last 6 sts, p5, k1.

10th row: *K5, p5; rep from * to end.

Rep these 10 rows.

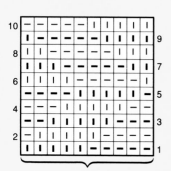

Rep these 10 sts

Polperro Laughing Boy

Multiple of 6 sts + 4.

1st row (right side): Knit.

2nd row: Purl.

3rd row: Knit.

4th row: P4, *k2, p4; rep from * to end.

5th and 6th rows: Rep the last 2 rows once more.

7th and 8th rows: As 1st and 2nd rows.

Rep these 8 rows.

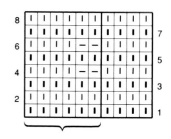

Rep these 6 sts

Diagonal Seed Stitch

Multiple of 6 sts + 6.

1st row (right side): *K5, p1; rep from * to end.

2nd row: P1, *k1, p5; rep from * to last 5 sts, k1, p4.

3rd row: K3, *p1, k5; rep from * to last 3 sts, p1, k2.

4th row: P3, *k1, p5; rep from * to last 3 sts, k1, p2.

5th row: K1, *p1, k5; rep from * to last 5 sts, p1, k4.

6th row: *P5, k1; rep from * to end.

Rep these 6 rows.

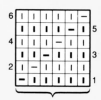

Rep these 6 sts

Reverse Stocking Stitch Chevrons

Multiple of 6 sts + 5.

1st row (right side): K5, *p1, k5; rep from * to end.

2nd row: K1, *p3, k3; rep from * to last 4 sts, p3, k1.

3rd row: P2, *k1, p2; rep from * to end.

4th row: P1, *k3, p3; rep from * to last 4 sts, k3, p1.

5th row: K2, *p1, k5; rep from * to last 3 sts, p1, k2.

6th row: Purl.

Rep these 6 rows.

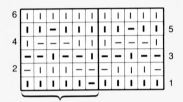

Rep these 6 sts

Lattice Stitch

Multiple of 6 sts + 7.

1st row (right side): K3, p1, *k5, p1; rep from * to last 3 sts, k3.

2nd row: P2, k1, p1, k1, *p3, k1, p1, k1; rep from * to last 2 sts, p2.

3rd row: K1, *p1, k3, p1, k1; rep from * to end.

4th row: K1, *p5, k1; rep from * to end.

5th row: As 3rd row.

6th row: As 2nd row.

Rep these 6 rows.

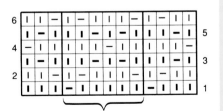

Rep these 6 sts

Piqué Rib

Multiple of 10 sts + 3 .

1st row (right side): K3, *p3, k1, p3, k3; rep from * to end.

2nd row: P3, *k3, p1, k3, p3; rep from * to end.

3rd row: As 1st row.

4th row: Knit.

Rep these 4 rows.

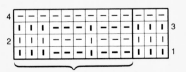

Rep these 10 sts

All-over Textures

Little Arrows

Multiple of 8 sts + 9.

1st row (right side): K1, *p1, k5, p1, k1; rep from * to end.

2nd row: P1, *k2, p3, k2, p1; rep from * to end.

3rd row: K2, p2, k1, p2, *k3, p2, k1, p2; rep from * to last 2 sts, k2.

4th row: P3, k1, p1, k1, *p5, k1, p1, k1; rep from * to last 3 sts, p3.

Rep these 4 rows.

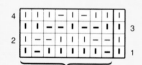

Rep these 8 sts

Dotted Ladder Stitch

Multiple of 8 sts + 5.

1st row (right side): K2, p1, k2, *p3, k2, p1, k2; rep from * to end.

2nd row: [P1, k1] twice, p1, *k3, [p1, k1] twice, p1; rep from * to end.

3rd and 4th rows: Rep these 2 rows once more.

5th row: K1, *p3, k2, p1, k2; rep from * to last 4 sts, p3, k1.

6th row: P1, k3, p1, *[k1, p1] twice, k3, p1; rep from * to end.

7th and 8th rows: Rep the last 2 rows once more.

Rep these 8 rows.

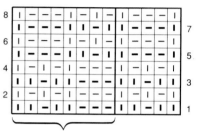

Rep these 8 sts

Spiral Pattern

Multiple of 7 sts + 7.

1st row (right side): P2, k4, *p3, k4; rep from * to last st, p1.

2nd row: K1, p3, *k4, p3; rep from * to last 3 sts, k3.

3rd row: P1, k1, p2, *k2, p2, k1, p2; rep from * to last 3 sts, k2, p1.

4th row: K1, p1, k2, p2, *k2, p1, k2, p2; rep from * to last st, k1.

5th row: P1, k3, *p4, k3; rep from * to last 3 sts, p3.

6th row: K2, p4, *k3, p4; rep from * to last st, k1.

7th row: P1, k5, *p2, k5; rep from * to last st, p1.

8th row: K1, p5, *k2, p5; rep from * to last st, k1.

Rep these 8 rows.

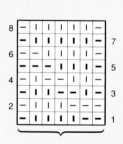

Rep these 7 sts

Mosaic Stitch

Multiple of 10 sts + 7.

1st row (right side): P3, *k1, p3, k1, p1, k1, p3; rep from * to last 4 sts, k1, p3.

2nd row: K3, *p1, k3, p1, k1, p1, k3; rep from * to last 4 sts, p1, k3.

3rd and 4th rows: Rep these 2 rows once more.

5th row: P2, *k1, p1, [k1, p3] twice; rep from * to last 5 sts, k1, p1, k1, p2.

6th row: K2, *p1, k1, [p1, k3] twice; rep from * to last 5 sts, p1, k1, p1, k2.

7th and 8th rows: Rep the last 2 rows once more.

Rep these 8 rows.

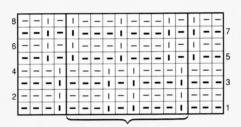

Rep these 10 sts

Small Basket Stitch

Multiple of 10 sts + 15.

1st row (right side): [K1, p1] twice, *k7, p1, k1, p1; rep from * to last st, k1.

2nd row: P1, [k1, p1] twice, *k5, [p1, k1] twice, p1; rep from * to end.

3rd and 4th rows: Rep these 2 rows once more.

5th row: K6, *p1, k1, p1, k7; rep from * to last 9 sts, p1, k1, p1, k6.

6th row: *K5, [p1, k1] twice, p1; rep from * to last 5 sts, k5.

7th and 8th rows: Rep the last 2 rows once more.

Rep these 8 rows.

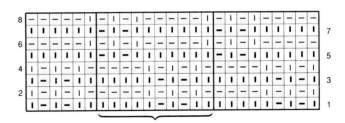

Rep these 10 sts

All-over Texture

Moss Stitch Zigzag

Multiple of 9 sts + 9.

1st row (right side): *[K1, p1] twice, k4, p1; rep from * to end.

2nd row: *P4, [k1, p1] twice, k1; rep from * to end.

3rd row: [K1, p1] 3 times, *k4, [p1, k1] twice, p1; rep from * to last 3 sts, k3.

4th row: P2, *[k1, p1] twice, k1, p4; rep from * to last 7 sts, [k1, p1] twice, k1, p2.

5th row: K3, *[p1, k1] twice, p1, k4; rep from * to last 6 sts, [p1, k1] 3 times.

6th row: *[K1, p1] twice, k1, p4; rep from * to end.

7th row: As 5th row.

8th row: As 4th row.

9th row: As 3rd row.

10th row: As 2nd row.

Rep these 10 rows.

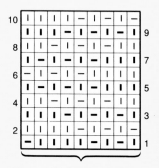

Rep these 9 sts

Chequerboard

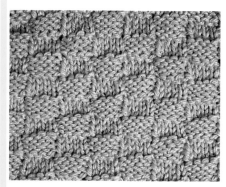

Multiple of 8 sts + 4.

1st row (right side): K4, *p4, k4; rep from * to end.

2nd row: P4, *k4, p4; rep from * to end.

3rd and 4th rows: Rep these 2 rows once more.

5th row: P4, *k4, p4; rep from * to end.

6th row: K4, *p4, k4; rep from * to end.

7th and 8th rows: Rep the last 2 rows once more.

Rep these 8 rows.

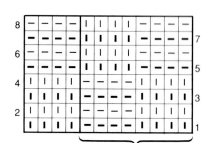

Rep these 8 sts

Moss Panels

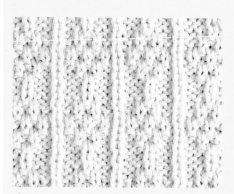

Multiple of 8 sts + 7.

1st row (wrong side): K3, *p1, k3; rep from * to end.

2nd row: P3, *k1, p3; rep from * to end.

3rd row: K2, p1, k1, *[p1, k2] twice, p1, k1; rep from * to last 3 sts, p1, k2.

4th row: P2, k1, p1, *[k1, p2] twice, k1, p1; rep from * to last 3 sts, k1, p2.

5th row: K1, *p1, k1; rep from * to end.

6th row: P1, *k1, p1; rep from * to end.

7th and 8th rows: As 3rd and 4th rows.

9th and 10th rows: As 1st and 2nd rows.

Rep these 10 rows.

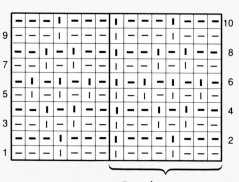

Rep these 8 sts

KNITTING
starting
STITCHES

3

Child's play ...

Here are a cotton t-shirt and a baby's blanket - made of squares and rectangles - and some colourful slip stitch patterns.

All-over Patterns

Textured Stripe

Multiple of 3 sts + 3.

1st row (right side): Knit.

2nd row: Purl.

3rd and 4th rows: Rep these 2 rows once more.

5th row: K1, *p1, k2; rep from * to last 2 sts, p1, k1.

6th row: P1, *k1, p2; rep from * to last 2 sts, k1, p1.

7th and 8th rows: Rep the last 2 rows once more.

9th row: *P2, k1; rep from * to end.

10th row: *P1, k2; rep from * to end.

11th and 12th rows: Rep the last 2 rows once more.

Rep these 12 rows.

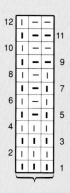

Rep these 3 sts

Broken Rib Diagonal

Multiple of 6 sts + 6.

1st row (right side): *K4, p2; rep from * to end.

2nd row: *K2, p4; rep from * to end.

3rd and 4th rows: Rep these 2 rows once more.

5th row: K2, *p2, k4; rep from * to last 4 sts, p2, k2.

6th row: P2, *k2, p4; rep from * to last 4 sts, k2, p2.

7th and 8th rows: Rep the last 2 rows once more.

9th row: *P2, k4; rep from * to end.

10th row: *P4, k2; rep from * to end.

11th and 12th rows: Rep the last 2 rows once more.

Rep these 12 rows.

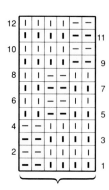

Rep these 6 sts

Pennant Stitch

Multiple of 5 sts.

1st row (right side): Knit.

2nd row: *K1, p4; rep from * to end.

3rd row: *K3, p2; rep from * to end.

4th row: *K3, p2; rep from * to end.

5th row: *K1, p4; rep from * to end.

6th row: Knit.

7th row: Knit.

8th row: *P4, k1; rep from * to end.

9th row: *P2, k3; rep from * to end.

10th row: *P2, k3; rep from * to end.

11th row: *P4, k1; rep from * to end.

12th row: Knit.

Rep these 12 rows.

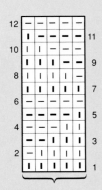

Rep these 5 sts

Polperro Northcott

Multiple of 4 sts + 2.

1st row (right side): Knit.

2nd row: Purl.

3rd, 4th and 5th rows: Knit.

6th row: P2, *k2, p2; rep from * to end.

7th row: Knit.

8th to 27th rows: Rep the last 2 rows 10 times more.

28th row: Knit.

Rep these 28 rows.

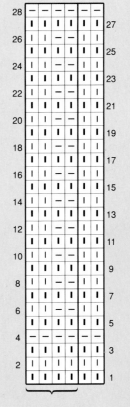

Rep these 4 sts

For information about Measuring-Tension/Gauge over Stitch Patterns refer to page 20.

All-over Patterns

Spiral Rib

Multiple of 6 sts + 3.

1st row (right side): K3, *p3, k3; rep from * to end.

2nd row: P3, *k3, p3; rep from * to end.

3rd row: As 1st row.

4th row: K1, *p3, k3; rep from * to last 2 sts, p2.

5th row: K2, *p3, k3; rep from * to last st, p1.

6th row: As 4th row.

7th row: K1, *p3, k3; rep from * to last 2 sts, p2.

8th row: K2, *p3, k3; rep from * to last st, p1.

9th row: As 7th row.

10th row: K3, *p3, k3; rep from * to end.

11th row: P3, *k3, p3; rep from * to end.

12th row: As 10th row.

13th row: P2, *k3, p3; rep from * to last st, k1.

14th row: P1, *k3, p3; rep from * to last 2 sts, k2.

15th row: As 13th row.

16th row: P2, *k3, p3; rep from * to last st, k1.

17th row: P1, *k3, p3; rep from * to last 2 sts, k2.

18th row: As 16th row.

Rep these 18 rows.

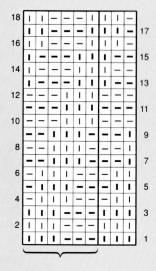

Rep these 6 sts

Zigzag Moss Stitch

Multiple of 6 sts + 7.

1st row (right side): Knit.

2nd row: Purl.

3rd row: P1, *k5, p1; rep from * to end.

4th row: P1, *k1, p3, k1, p1; rep from * to end.

5th row: P1, *k1, p1; rep from * to end.

6th row: P1, *k1, p1; rep from * to end.

7th row: K2, p1, k1, p1, *k3, p1, k1, p1; rep from * to last 2 sts, k2.

8th row: P3, k1, *p5, k1; rep from * to last 3 sts, p3.

9th and 10th rows: As 1st and 2nd rows.

11th row: K3, p1, *k5, p1; rep from * to last 3 sts, k3.

12th row: P2, k1, p1, k1, *p3, k1, p1, k1; rep from * to last 2 sts, p2.

13th row: K1, *p1, k1; rep from * to end.

14th row: K1, *p1, k1; rep from * to end.

15th row: K1, *p1, k3, p1, k1; rep from * to end.

16th row: K1, *p5, k1; rep from * to end.

Rep these 16 rows.

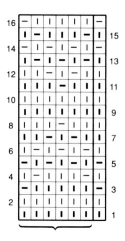

Rep these 6 sts

Lizard Lattice

Multiple of 6 sts + 3.

1st row (right side): Knit.

2nd row: Purl.

3rd and 4th rows: Rep these 2 rows once more.

5th row: P3, *k3, p3; rep from * to end.

6th row: Purl.

7th to 10th rows: Rep the last 2 rows twice more.

11th and 12th rows: As 1st and 2nd rows.

13th row: Knit.

14th row: P3, *k3, p3; rep from * to end.

15th to 18th rows: Rep the last 2 rows twice more.

Rep these 18 rows.

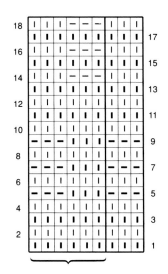

Rep these 6 sts

Diamond Web

Multiple of 6 sts + 7.

1st row (right side): P3, *k1, p5; rep from * to last 4 sts, k1, p3.

2nd row: K3, *p1, k5; rep from * to last 4 sts, p1, k3.

3rd and 4th rows: Rep these 2 rows once more.

5th row: P2, *k1, p1, k1, p3; rep from * to last 5 sts, k1, p1, k1, p2.

6th row: K2, *p1, k1, p1, k3; rep from * to last 5 sts, p1, k1, p1, k2.

7th and 8th rows: Rep the last 2 rows once more.

9th row: P1, *k1, p3, k1, p1; rep from * to end.

10th row: K1, *p1, k3, p1, k1; rep from * to end.

11th and 12th rows: Rep the last 2 rows once more.

13th row: K1, *p5, k1; rep from * to end.

14th row: P1, *k5, p1; rep from * to end.

15th and 16th rows: Rep the last 2 rows once more.

17th to 20th rows: Rep 9th and 10th rows twice.

21st to 24th rows: Rep 5th and 6th rows twice.

Rep these 24 rows.

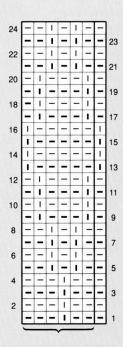

Rep these 6 sts

Child's T-Shirt

Measurements

	50/55	60/65	70/75	
To fit chest size	20/22	24/26	28/30	ins
Finished measurement	60	70	79	cm
	24	28	31½	ins
Length to shoulder	36	42	48	cm
(approximately)	14¼	16½	19	ins
Sleeve length	13	15	17	cm
	5	6	6½	ins

Shown in 60/65 cm [24/26 inch] size.

Materials
Cotton Double Knitting yarn

	250	300	400	grams
	9	11	15	ounces

Pair needles each size 3¼ mm (UK 10, USA 3 or 4) and 4mm (UK 8, USA 6). 4 buttons.

The quantities of yarn stated are based on average requirements and are therefore approximate.
For abbreviations see page 24.

Tension

21 sts and 31 rows = 10 cm [4 ins] square measured over pattern using larger needles.

Back and Front (Alike)

Using smaller needles cast on 63(73-83) sts.

1st row: K1, *p1, k1; rep from * to end.

This row forms the moss stitch. Rep this row 4 more times.
Change to larger needles and purl 1 row (wrong side).
Commence pattern.

1st row: K6, p1, *k9, p1; rep from * to last 6 sts, k6.

2nd row: P5, k1, p1, k1, *p7, k1, p1, k1; rep from * to last 5 sts, p5.

3rd row: K4, [p1, k1] twice, p1, *k5, p1, [k1, p1] twice; rep from * to last 4 sts, k4.

4th row: P3, *[k1, p1] 3 times, k1, p3; rep from * to end.

5th row: P1, *k1, p1; rep from * to end.

6th row: As 4th row.

7th row: As 3rd row.

8th row: As 2nd row.

9th row: As 1st row.

10th row: Purl.

These 10 rows form the pattern. Continue in pattern until piece measures approximately 34(40-48) cm [13½ (16-19¼)ins] ending with a 5th or 9th row of pattern. Purl 1 row.

Change to smaller needles and work 5 rows in moss stitch as given at beg. Cast off in moss stitch.

Sleeves

Using smaller needles cast on 63(63-73) sts and work 5 rows in moss stitch as given for Back and Front.

Change to larger needles and purl 1 row (wrong side). Work 13(15-17) cm [5(6-6½) ins] in pattern as given for Back and Front ending with a wrong side row. Cast off.

To Finish

Press pieces according to instructions on ball band.

Join shoulder seams across 8 sts at either side. Fold each sleeve in half lengthways and mark centre of cast off edge. Sew each sleeve to a side edge placing centre at shoulder seam. **Note:** Armholes should measure approximately 13(15-17) cm [5¼(6-6¾ ins]. Join side and sleeve seams. Make 2 button loops on each front shoulder edge, the first button loop 4 cm [1½ ins] from shoulder seam and the second halfway between first button loop and shoulder seam. Sew buttons on back shoulder edges to correspond.

To make a button loop

Fasten yarn just under edge and take it to the right the same distance as diameter of button; catch in edge of knitting, then return to starting point and catch in edge again. Work buttonhole stitch closely over these two threads as shown.

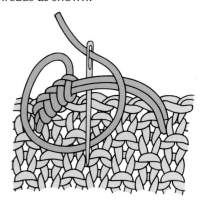

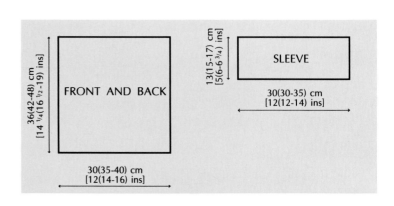

FRONT AND BACK

36(42-48) cm [14¼(16½-19) ins]

30(35-40) cm [12(14-16) ins]

SLEEVE

13(15-17) cm [5(6-6¾) ins]

30(30-35) cm [12(12-14) ins]

All-over Patterns

Moss Stitch Triangles

Multiple of 8 sts + 8.

1st row (right side): *P1, k7; rep from * to end.

2nd row: P6, *k1, p7; rep from * to last 2 sts, k1, p1.

3rd row: *P1, k1, p1, k5; rep from * to end.

4th row: P4, *k1, p1, k1, p5; rep from * to last 4 sts, [k1, p1] twice.

5th row: *[P1, k1] twice, p1, k3; rep from * to end.

6th row: P2, *[k1, p1] twice, k1, p3; rep from * to last 6 sts, [k1, p1] 3 times.

7th row: *P1, k1; rep from * to end.

8th row: As 6th row.

9th row: As 5th row.

10th row: As 4th row.

11th row: As 3rd row.

12th row: As 2nd row.

Rep these 12 rows.

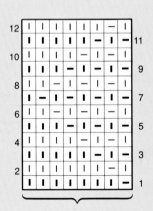

Rep these 8 sts

Broken Diagonal Check

Multiple of 8 sts + 8.

1st row (right side): *K6, p2; rep from * to end.

2nd row: P1, *k2, p6; rep from * to last 7 sts, k2, p5.

3rd row: K4, *p2, k6; rep from * to last 4 sts, p2, k2.

4th row: P3, *k2, p6; rep from * to last 5 sts, k2, p3.

5th row: K2, *p2, k6; rep from * to last 6 sts, p2, k4.

6th row: P5, *k2, p6; rep from * to last 3 sts, k2, p1.

7th row: Purl.

8th row: K2, *p6, k2; rep from * to last 6 sts, p6.

9th row: K5, *p2, k6; rep from * to last 3 sts, p2, k1.

10th row: P2, *k2, p6; rep from * to last 6 sts, k2, p4.

11th row: K3, *p2, k6; rep from * to last 5 sts, p2, k3.

12th row: P4, *k2, p6; rep from * to last 4 sts, k2, p2.

13th row: K1, *p2, k6; rep from * to last 7 sts, p2, k5.

14th row: Knit.

Rep these 14 rows.

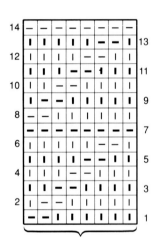

Rep these 8 sts

50

Steps

Multiple of 8 sts + 2.

1st row (right side): *K4, p4; rep from * to last 2 sts, k2.

2nd row: P2, *k4, p4; rep from * to end.

3rd and 4th rows: Rep these 2 rows once more.

5th row: K2, *p4, k4; rep from * to end.

6th row: *P4, k4; rep from * to last 2 sts, p2.

7th and 8th rows: Rep the last 2 rows once more.

9th row: *P4, k4; rep from * to last 2 sts, p2.

10th row: K2, *p4, k4; rep from * to end.

11th and 12th rows: Rep the last 2 rows once more.

13th row: P2, *k4, p4; rep from * to end.

14th row: *K4, p4; rep from * to last 2 sts, k2.

15th and 16th rows: Rep the last 2 rows once more.

Rep these 16 rows.

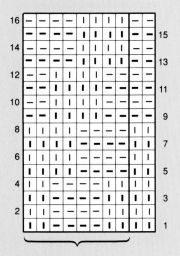

Rep these 8 sts

Triangle Ribs

Multiple of 8 sts.

1st row (right side): *P2, k6; rep from * to end.

2nd row: *P6, k2; rep from * to end.

3rd row: *P3, k5; rep from * to end.

4th row: *P4, k4; rep from * to end.

5th row: *P5, k3; rep from * to end.

6th row: *P2, k6; rep from * to end.

7th row: *P7, k1; rep from * to end.

8th row: *P2, k6; rep from * to end.

9th row: As 5th row.

10th row: As 4th row.

11th row: As 3rd row.

12th row: As 2nd row.

Rep these 12 rows.

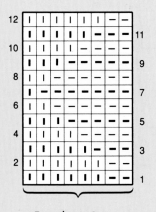

Rep these 8 sts

Measurement

Finished Blanket measures approximately 90 x 90 cm [36 x 36 ins] including edging.

Materials

4 ply knittting yarn

Colour A	150	grams
	5	ounces
Colour B	100	grams
	3	ounces
Colour C	150	grams
	5	ounces

Pair needles each size 3 1/4mm (UK 10, USA 3 or 4) and 2 3/4mm (UK 12, USA 2).

The quantities of yarn stated are based on average requirements and are therefore approximate.

For abbreviations see page 24.

Tension

30 sts and 45 rows = 10 cm [4 ins] square measured over slip stitch rib pattern using larger needles.

Slip Stitch Rib Square

(Make 13)

Using larger needles and A cast on 51 sts and purl 1 row. Commence pattern.

1st row (right side): Using B, k1, *yf, sl 1, yb, k1; rep from * to end.

2nd row: Using B, purl.

3rd row: Using A, k1, *yf, sl 1, yb, k1; rep from * to end.

4th row: Using A, purl.

These 4 rows form the pattern. Rep these 4 rows until piece measures 17 cm [6 3/4 ins] ending with a wrong side row. Cast off.

Diamond Pattern Square

(Make 12)

Using larger needles and C cast on 47 sts.

1st row (right side): P5, *k4, p1, k4, p5; rep from * to end.

2nd row: K5, *p3, k3, p3, k5; rep from * to end.

3rd row: K7, p5, [k9, p5] twice, k7.

4th row: P6, k7, [p7, k7] twice, p6.

5th row: K5, *p9, k5; rep from * to end.

6th row: As 4th row.

7th row: As 3rd row.

8th row: As 2nd row.

These 8 rows form the pattern. Rep these 8 rows until piece measures 17 cm [6 3/4 ins] ending with a 4th or 8th row of pattern. Cast off in pattern.

Finishing and Edging

Do not press.

Join squares as shown in diagram.

Edgings (Make 2 each in colours A and B)

Using smaller needles cast on 10 sts and work in garter st (every row knit) until piece measures 3 cm [1 1/4 ins] **more** than 1 edge of Blanket. Cast off.

Sew edgings in place as shown in diagram.

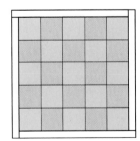

KEY

▨	=	Slip stitch rib square
▨	=	Diamond pattern square
☐	=	Edging A
☐	=	Edging B

Slip Stitch Patterns

Basket Rib I

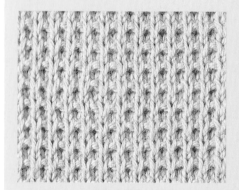

Multiple of 2 sts + 1.

1st row (right side): Knit.

2nd row: Purl.

3rd row: K1, *sl 1, k1; rep from * to end.

4th row: K1, *yf, sl 1, yb, k1; rep from * to end.

Rep these 4 rows.

Rep these 2 sts

Basket Rib II

Work as given for Basket Rib I **but** working 1st and 2nd pattern rows in A, 3rd and 4th rows in B throughout.

Basket Rib III

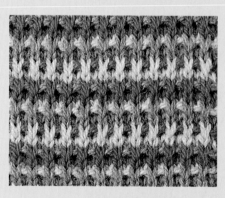

Work as given for Basket Rib I **but** working 1 row each in colours A, B and C throughout.

Woven Stitch I

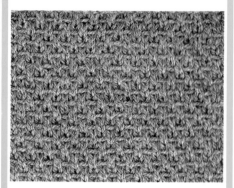

Multiple of 2 sts + 3.

Note: Slip sts purlwise with yarn at front (right side) of work, on right side rows = 🡓 on chart.

1st row (right side): K1, *yf, sl 1, yb, k1; rep from * to end.

2nd row: Purl.

3rd row: K2, *yf, sl 1, yb, k1; rep from * to last st, k1.

4th row: Purl.

Rep these 4 rows.

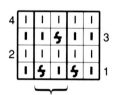

Rep these 2 sts

Woven Stitch II

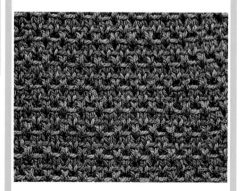

Work as given for Woven Stitch I **but** working 1st and 2nd rows in A, 3rd and 4th rows in B.

Double Woven Stitch I

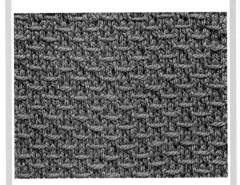

Multiple of 4 sts + 4.

Note: Slip sts purlwise with yarn at front (right side) of work, on right side rows = 🖏 on chart.

1st row (right side): K3, *yf, sl 2, yb, k2; rep from * to last st, k1.

2nd row: Purl.

3rd row: K1, *yf, sl 2, yb, k2; rep from * to last 3 sts, sl 2, k1.

4th row: Purl.

Rep these 4 rows.

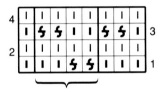

Rep these 4 sts

Double Woven Stitch II

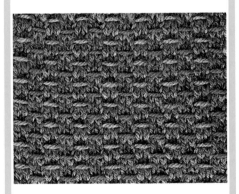

Work as given for Double Woven Stitch I **but** working 1st and 2nd rows in A, 3rd and 4th rows in B.

Moss Slip Stitch I

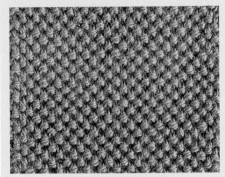

Multiple of 2 sts + 3.

1st row (right side): K1, *sl 1, k1; rep from * to end.

2nd row: K1, *yf, sl 1, yb, k1; rep from * to end.

3rd row: K2, *sl 1, k1; rep from * to last st, k1.

4th row: K2, *yf, sl 1, yb, k1; rep from * to last st, k1.

Rep these 4 rows.

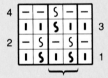

Rep these 2 sts

Moss Slip Stitch II

Work as given for Moss Slip Stitch I **but** working 1st and 2nd pattern rows in colour A, 3rd and 4th rows in B throughout.

Moss Slip Stitch III

Work as given for Moss Slip Stitch I **but** beginning with the 1st row, work 2 rows in colour A, 2 rows in B and 2 rows in C throughout.

Moss Slip Stitch IV

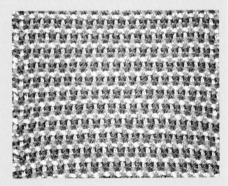

Work as given for Moss Slip Stitch I **but** working 1 row each in colours A, B and C throughout.

Slip Stitch Patterns

Speckle Rib I

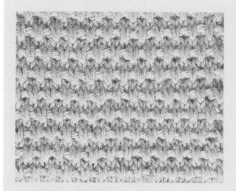

Multiple of 2 sts + 3.

1st row (right side): Knit.

2nd row: Purl.

3rd row: K1, *sl 1, k1; rep from * to end.

4th row: K1, *yf, sl 1, yb, k1; rep from * to end.

5th and 6th rows: As 1st and 2nd rows.

7th row: K2, *sl 1, k1; rep from * to last st, k1.

8th row: K2. *yf, sl 1, yb, k1; rep from * to last st, k1.

Rep these 8 rows.

Rep these 2 sts

Speckle Rib II

Work as given for Speckle Rib I **but** working 1st, 2nd, 5th and 6th rows in A, 3rd, 4th, 7th and 8th rows in B throughout.

Speckle Rib III

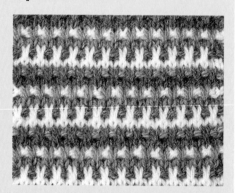

Work as given for Speckle Rib I **but** beginning with the 1st row, work 2 rows in colour A, 2 rows in B and 2 rows in C throughout.

Speckle Rib IV

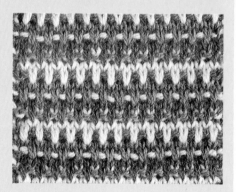

Work as given for Speckle Rib I **but** working 1 row each in colours A, B and C throughout.

Garter Slip Stitch I

Multiple of 2 sts + 1.

1st row (right side): Knit.

2nd row: Knit.

3rd row: K1, *sl 1, k1; rep from * to end.

4th row: K1, *yf, sl 1, yb, k1; rep from * to end.

Rep these 4 rows.

Rep these 2 sts

Garter Slip Stitch II

Work as given for Garter Slip Stitch I **but** working 1st and 2nd rows in A, 3rd and 4th rows in B throughout.

Garter Slip Stitch III

Work as given for Garter Slip Stitch I **but** beginning with the 1st row work 2 rows in colour A, 2 rows in B and 2 rows in C throughout.

Garter Slip Stitch IV

Work as given for Garter Slip Stitch I **but** working 1 row each in colours A, B and C throughout.

Slip Stitch Patterns

Garter Slip Stitch V

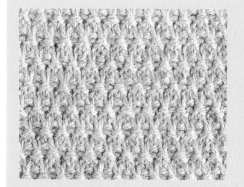

Multiple of 2 sts + 3.

1st row (right side): Knit.

2nd row: Knit.

3rd row: K1, *sl 1, k1; rep from * to end.

4th row: K1, *yf, sl 1, yb, k1; rep from * to end.

5th and 6th rows: As 1st and 2nd rows.

7th row: K2, *sl 1, k1; rep from * to last st, k1.

8th row: K2, *yf, sl 1, yb, k1; rep from * to last st, k1.

Rep these 8 rows.

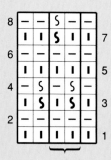

Rep these 2 sts

Garter Slip Stitch VI

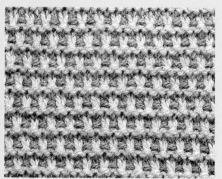

Work as given for Garter Slip Stitch V **but** working 1st, 2nd, 5th and 6th rows in A, 3rd, 4th, 7th and 8th rows in B throughout.

Garter Slip Stitch VII

Work as given for Garter Slip Stitch V **but** beginning with the 1st row work 2 rows in colour A, 2 rows in colour B and 2 rows in colour C throughout.

Garter Slip Stitch VIII

Work as given for Garter Slip Stitch V **but** working 1 row each in colours A, B and C throughout.

KNITTING
starting
STITCHES

4

Go for bold ...
> with a collection of large-scale patterns. Make a stylish tunic and matching tube skirt, or a classic cabled sweater for a man.

Textured Patterns

Garter Stitch Steps

Multiple of 8 sts + 8.

1st row (right side): Knit.

2nd row: *K4, p4; rep from * to end.

3rd and 4th rows: Rep these 2 rows once more.

5th row: Knit.

6th row: K2, *p4, k4; rep from * to last 6 sts, p4, k2.

7th and 8th rows: Rep the last 2 rows once more.

9th row: Knit.

10th row: *P4, k4; rep from * to end.

11th and 12th rows: Rep the last 2 rows once more.

13th row: Knit.

14th row: P2, *k4, p4; rep from * to last 6 sts, k4, p2.

15th and 16th rows: Rep the last 2 rows once more.

Rep these 16 rows.

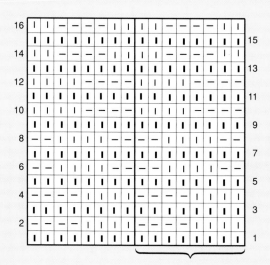

Rep these 8 sts

Chevron

Multiple of 8 sts + 9.

1st row (right side): K1, *p7, k1; rep from * to end.

2nd row: P1, *k7, p1; rep from * to end.

3rd row: K2, *p5, k3; rep from * to last 7 sts, p5, k2.

4th row: P2, *k5, p3; rep from * to last 7 sts, k5, p2.

5th row: K3, *p3, k5; rep from * to last 6 sts, p3, k3.

6th row: P3, *k3, p5; rep from * to last 6 sts, k3, p3.

7th row: K4, *p1, k7; rep from * to last 5 sts, p1, k4.

8th row: P4, *k1, p7; rep from * to last 5 sts, k1, p4.

9th row: P1, *k7, p1; rep from * to end.

10th row: K1, *p7, k1; rep from * to end.

11th row: P2, *k5, p3; rep from * to last 7 sts, k5, p2.

12th row: K2, *p5, k3; rep from * to last 7 sts, p5, k2.

13th row: P3, *k3, p5; rep from * to last 6 sts, k3, p3.

14th row: K3, *p3, k5; rep from * to last 6 sts, p3, k3.

15th row: P4, *k1, p7; rep from * to last 5 sts, k1, p4.

16th row: K4, *p1, k7; rep from * to last 5 sts, p1, k4.

Rep these 16 rows.

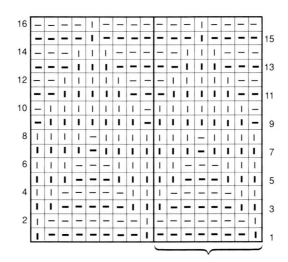

Rep these 8 sts

Enlarged Basket Stitch

Multiple of 18 sts + 10.

1st row (right side): K11, *p2, k2, p2, k12; rep from * to last 17 sts, p2, k2, p2, k11.

2nd row: P1, *k8, [p2, k2] twice, p2; rep from * to last 9 sts, k8, p1.

3rd row: K1, *p8, [k2, p2] twice, k2; rep from * to last 9 sts, p8, k1.

4th row: P11, *k2, p2, k2, p12; rep from * to last 17 sts, k2, p2, k2, p11.

5th to 8th rows: Rep these 4 rows once more.

9th row: Knit.

10th row: [P2, k2] twice, p12, *k2, p2, k2, p12; rep from * to last 8 sts, [k2, p2] twice.

11th row: [K2, p2] twice, k2, *p8, [k2, p2] twice, k2; rep from * to end.

12th row: [P2, k2] twice, p2, *k8, [p2, k2] twice, p2; rep from * to end.

13th row: [K2, p2] twice, k12, *p2, k2, p2, k12; rep from * to last 8 sts, [p2, k2] twice.

14th to 17th rows: Rep the last 4 rows once more.

18th row: Purl.

Rep these 18 rows.

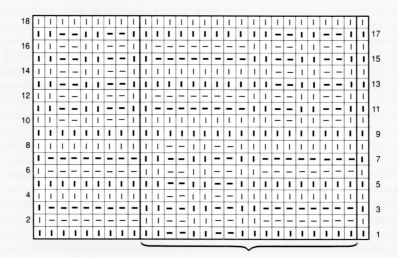

Rep these 18 sts

Elongated Chevron

Multiple of 18 sts + 1.

1st row (right side): P1, *[k2, p2] twice, k1, [p2, k2] twice, p1; rep from * to end.

2nd row: K1, *[p2, k2] twice, p1, [k2, p2] twice, k1; rep from * to end.

3rd and 4th rows: Rep these 2 rows once more.

5th row: [P2, k2] twice, *p3, k2, p2, k2; rep from * to last 2 sts, p2.

6th row: [K2, p2] twice, *k3, p2, k2, p2; rep from * to last 2 sts, k2.

7th and 8th rows: Rep the last 2 rows once more.

9th row: K1, *[p2, k2] twice, p1, [k2, p2] twice, k1; rep from * to end.

10th row: P1, *[k2, p2] twice, k1, [p2, k2] twice, p1; rep from * to end.

11th and 12th rows: Rep the last 2 rows once more.

13th row: [K2, p2] twice, *k3, p2, k2, p2; rep from * to last 2 sts, k2.

14th row: [P2, k2] twice, *p3, k2, p2, k2; rep from * to last 2 sts, p2.

15th and 16th rows: Rep the last 2 rows once more.

Rep these 16 rows.

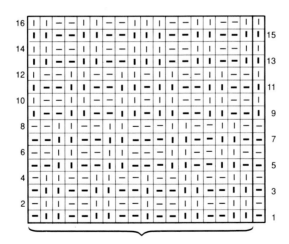

Rep these 18 sts

Woman's Sweater and Skirt

Measurements

Sweater

	75/80	85/90	95/100	cm
To fit bust size	30/32	34/36	38/40	ins
Finished measurement	99	110	121	cm
	39½	44	48½	ins
Length to shoulder	72	76	80	cm
	28¼	30	31½	ins
Sleeve length	43	43	43	cm
(excluding cuff turn back)	17	17	17	ins

Skirt

	80/85	90/95	100/105	cm
To fit hip size	32/34	36/38	40/42	ins
Length (excluding	43	43	43	cm
waistband), adjustable	17	17	17	ins

Both garments shown in 85/90 cm [34/36 inch] size.

Materials

Double Knitting yarn

Sweater	575	650	750	grams
	21	24	27	ounces
Skirt	325	350	400	grams
	12	13	15	ounces

Pair needles each size 4mm (UK 8, USA 6) and 3¼ mm (UK 10, USA 3 or 4).

2.5 cm [1 inch] wide elastic for waist of skirt.

The quantities of yarn stated are based on average requirements and are therefore approximate.
For abbreviations see page 24.

Tension

22 sts and 30 rows = 10 cm [4 ins] square measured over st st using larger needles.

Sweater

Back and Front (Alike)

Using smaller needles cast on 109(121-133) sts and work 5 rows in garter st (every row knit).
Change to larger needles and work 4 rows in st st starting knit.
Commence border pattern.
1st row (right side): K2, p1, k7, p1, *k3, p1, k7, p1; rep from * to last 2 sts, k2.
2nd row: P3, *k1, p5; rep from * to last 4 sts, k1, p3.
3rd row: K2, p1, k1, p1, *k3, p1, k1, p1; rep from * to last 2 sts, k2.
4th row: P3, k1, [p1, k1] 3 times, *p5, k1, [p1, k1] 3 times; rep from * to last 3 sts, p3.
5th row: K4, p1, [k1, p1] twice, *k7, p1, [k1, p1] twice; rep from * to last 4 sts, k4.
6th row: P5, k1, p1, k1, *p9, k1, p1, k1; rep from * to last 5 sts, p5.
7th row: As 5th row.
8th row: As 4th row.
9th row: As 3rd row.
10th row: As 2nd row.
11th row: As 1st row.
Work 3 rows in st st starting purl, then work 4 rows in garter st.
These 18 rows form border pattern.
Continue in st st, starting knit, until back measures 68(72-76) cm [26¾ (28¼ -30) ins] ending with a purl row. Work 4 cm [1½ ins] in garter st ending with a right side row. Cast off knitwise.

Sleeves

Using smaller needles cast on 50(50-56) sts.
1st row: K3, p2, *k4, p2; rep from * to last 3 sts, k3.
2nd row: P3, k2, *p4, k2; rep from * to last 3 sts, p3.
Rep these 2 rows until rib measures 16 cm [6¼ ins] ending with a 2nd row.
Next row (increase): *P4(4-3), purl into front and back of next st, p3(3-2); rep from * to last 6(6-5) sts, purl into front and back of next st p2(2-1). 61(61-73) sts.
Change to larger needles and work 4 rows in st st, starting knit. Work the 18 rows of border pattern as given for Back and Front.
Working in st st, starting knit, increase 1 st (by knitting into front and back of st) at each end of next and every alt row until there are 85(93-95) sts, then inc 1 st at each end of every 4th row until there are 107(111-117) sts. Work straight until sleeve measures 51 cm [20 ins] or 8 cm [3 ins] more than required length (for cuff turn back) ending with a purl row. Cast off.

To Finish

Press according to instructions on page 22.
Join shoulder seams leaving 23(25-27) cm [9(9¾-10½) ins] open at centre. Fold each sleeve in half lengthways and mark centre of cast off edge. Sew each sleeve to a side edge placing centre at shoulder seam. Join side and sleeve seams, reversing seam on lower half of rib to allow for turnback. Press seams.

Skirt

Back and Front (Alike)

Using larger needles cast on 122(140-152) sts.
1st row (right side): K3, p2, *k4, p2; rep from * to last 3 sts, k3.
2nd row: P3, k2, *p4, k2; rep from * to last 3 sts, p3.
Rep these 2 rows until Skirt measures 43 cm [17 ins] or required length ending with a wrong side row.
Change to smaller needles and work a further 6 cm [2½ ins] in rib ending with a wrong side row. Cast off loosely.

To Finish

Do not press.
Join side seams. Turn over 3 cm [1¼ ins] at waist to form casing for elastic and slip-stitch **loosely** in place leaving a small opening. Thread elastic through casing, adjust length to fit waist and join ends. Close opening.

23(25-27) cm
[9 (9¾-10½) ins]

72(76-80) cm
[28¼ (29¾-31½) ins]

BACK AND FRONT

50(55-61) cm
[20(22-24½) ins]

49(51-53) cm
[19½(20½-21¼) ins]

43 cm
[17 ins]

SLEEVE

35 cm
[13¾ ins]

28(28-33) cm
[11¼(11¼-13¼) ins]

16 cm
[6¼ ins]

46 cm
[18¼ ins]

SKIRT
BACK AND FRONT

6 cm
[2½ ins]

43 cm
[17 ins]

56(64-69) cm
[22½(25½-27½) ins]

Textured Patterns

Repeating Diamonds

Multiple of 22 sts + 23.

1st row (right side): K2, *p2, k2, p1, k3, p1, k1, p1, k3, p1, k2, p2, k3; rep from * to last 21 sts, p2, k2, p1, k3, p1, k1, p1, k3, p1, k2, p2, k2.

2nd row: P2, *k2, p2, k5, p1, k5, p2, k2, p3; rep from * to last 21 sts, k2, p2, k5, p1, k5, p2, k2, p2.

3rd and 4th rows: Rep these 2 rows once more.

5th row: K1, *p2, k2, [p1, k3] 3 times, p1, k2, p2, k1; rep from * to end.

6th row: P1, *k2, p2, k5, p3, k5, p2, k2, p1; rep from * to end.

7th and 8th rows: Rep the last 2 rows once more.

9th row: P2, *k2, p1, k3, [p1, k2] twice, p1, k3, p1, k2, p3; rep from * to last 21 sts, k2, p1, k3, [p1, k2] twice, p1, k3, p1, k2, p2.

10th row: K2, *p2, k5, p2, k1, p2, k5, p2, k3; rep from * to last 21 sts, p2, k5, p2, k1, p2, k5, p2, k2.

11th and 12th rows: Rep the last 2 rows once more.

13th row: P1, *k2, p1, k3, p1, k2, p3, k2, p1, k3, p1, k2, p1; rep from * to end.

14th row: K1, *p2, k5, p2, k3, p2, k5, p2, k1; rep from * to end.

15th and 16th rows: Rep the last 2 rows once more.

17th row: K2, *p1, k3, p1, k2, p2, k1, p2, k2, p1, k3, p1, k3; rep from * to last 21 sts, p1, k3, p1, k2, p2, k1, p2, k2, p1, k3, p1, k2.

18th row: P2, *k5, p2, k2, p1, k2, p2, k5, p3; rep from * to last 21 sts, k5, p2, k2, p1, k2, p2, k5, p2.

19th and 20th rows: Rep the last 2 rows once more.

21st row: K1, *p1, k3, p1, k2, p2, k3, p2, k2, p1, k3, p1, k1; rep from * to end.

22nd row: P1, *k5, p2, k2, p3, k2, p2, k5, p1; rep from * to end.

23rd and 24th rows: Rep the last 2 rows once more.

25th to 28th rows: Rep 17th and 18th rows twice.

29th to 32nd rows: Rep 13th and 14th rows twice.

33rd to 36th rows: Rep 9th and 10th rows twice.

37th to 40th rows: Rep 5th and 6th rows twice.

Rep these 40 rows.

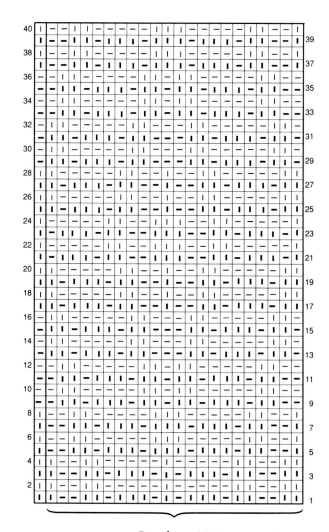

Rep these 22 sts

Staircase Pattern I

Multiple of 16 sts + 16.

1st row (right side): Knit.

2nd row: Purl.

3rd row: *K5, p11; rep from * to end.

4th row: *K11, p5; rep from * to end.

5th row: As 3rd row.

6th row: Purl.

7th and 8th rows: As 1st and 2nd rows.

9th row: P4, *k5, p11; rep from * to last 12 sts, k5, p7.

10th row: K7, *p5, k11; rep from * to last 9 sts, p5, k4.

11th row: As 9th row.

12th row: Purl.

13th and 14th rows: As 1st and 2nd rows.

15th row: P8, *k5, p11; rep from * to last 8 sts, k5, p3.

16th row: K3, *p5, k11; rep from * to last 13 sts, p5, k8.

17th row: As 15th row.

18th row: Purl.

19th and 20th rows: As 1st and 2nd rows.

21st row: K1, p11, *k5, p11; rep from * to last 4 sts, k4.

22nd row: P4, *k11, p5; rep from * to last 12 sts, k11, p1.

23rd row: As 21st row.

24th row: Purl.

Rep these 24 rows.

Rep these 16 sts

Staircase Pattern II

Work as given for Staircase Pattern I, using reverse side as right side.

Textured Patterns

Windmill Pattern

Multiple of 20 sts.

1st row (right side): *K10, p10; rep from * to end.

2nd row: *K9, p1, k1, p9; rep from * to end.

3rd row: *K8, p2, k2, p8; rep from * to end.

4th row: *K7, p3, k3, p7; rep from * to end.

5th row: *K6, p4, k4, p6; rep from * to end.

6th row: *K5, p5; rep from * to end.

7th row: *K4, p6, k6, p4; rep from * to end.

8th row: *K3, p7, k7, p3; rep from * to end.

9th row: *K2, p8, k8, p2; rep from * to end.

10th row: *K1, p9, k9, p1; rep from * to end.

11th row: *P10, k10; rep from * to end.

12th row: *K10, p10; rep from * to end.

13th row: *P1, k9, p9, k1; rep from * to end.

14th row: *P2, k8, p8, k2; rep from * to end.

15th row: *P3, k7, p7, k3; rep from * to end.

16th row: *P4, k6, p6, k4; rep from * to end.

17th row: *P5, k5; rep from * to end.

18th row: *P6, k4, p4, k6; rep from * to end.

19th row: *P7, k3, p3, k7; rep from * to end.

20th row: *P8, k2, p2, k8; rep from * to end.

21st row: *P9, k1, p1, k9; rep from * to end.

22nd row: *P10, k10; rep from * to end.

Rep these 22 rows.

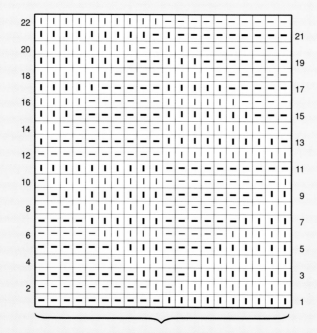

Rep these 20 sts

Chevron Stripes

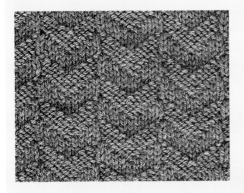

Multiple of 18 sts + 9.

1st row (right side): P4, k1, p4, *k4, p1, k4, p4, k1, p4; rep from * to end.

2nd row: K3, *p3, k3; rep from * to end.

3rd row: P2, k5, p2, *k2, p5, k2, p2, k5, p2; rep from * to end.

4th row: K1, p7, k1, *p1, k7, p1, k1, p7, k1; rep from * to end.

5th row: K4, p1, k4, *p4, k1, p4, k4, p1, k4; rep from * to end.

6th row: P3, *k3, p3; rep from * to end.

7th row: K2, p5, k2, *p2, k5, p2, k2, p5, k2; rep from * to end.

8th row: P1, k7, p1, *k1, p7, k1, p1, k7, p1; rep from * to end.

Rep these 8 rows.

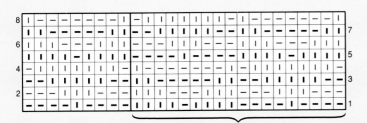

Rep these 18 sts

Moss Diamonds

Multiple of 10 sts + 7.

1st row (right side): *[K3, p1] twice, k1, p1; rep from * to last 7 sts, k3, p1, k3.

2nd row: *[P3, k1] twice, p1, k1; rep from * to last 7 sts, p3, k1, p3.

3rd row: K2, p1, k1, p1, *[k3, p1] twice, k1, p1; rep from * to last 2 sts, k2.

4th row: P2, k1, p1, k1, *[p3, k1] twice, p1, k1; rep from * to last 2 sts, p2.

5th row: [K1, p1] 3 times, *[k2, p1] twice, [k1, p1] twice; rep from * to last st, k1.

6th row: [P1, k1] 3 times, *[p2, k1] twice, [p1, k1] twice; rep from * to last st, p1.

7th and 8th rows: As 3rd and 4th rows.

9th and 10th rows: As 1st and 2nd rows.

11th row: K3, p1, *k2, [p1, k1] twice, p1, k2, p1; rep from * to last 3 sts, k3.

12th row: P3, k1, *p2, [k1, p1] twice, k1, p2, k1; rep from * to last 3 sts, p3.

Rep these 12 rows.

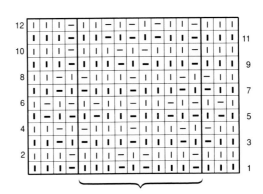

Rep these 10 sts

Textured Patterns

Fancy Diamond Pattern

Multiple of 15 sts + 15.

1st row (right side): K1, *p13, k2; rep from * to last 14 sts, p13, k1.

2nd row: P2, *k11, p4; rep from * to last 13 sts, k11, p2.

3rd row: K3, *p9, k6; rep from * to last 12 sts, p9, k3.

4th row: P4, *k7, p8; rep from * to last 11 sts, k7, p4.

5th row: K5, *p5, k10; rep from * to last 10 sts, p5, k5.

6th row: K1, *p5, k3, p5, k2; rep from * to last 14 sts, p5, k3, p5, k1.

7th row: P2, *k5, p1, k5, p4; rep from * to last 13 sts, k5, p1, k5, p2.

8th row: K3, *p9, k6; rep from * to last 12 sts, p9, k3.

9th row: As 7th row.

10th row: As 6th row.

11th row: As 5th row.

12th row: As 4th row.

13th row: As 3rd row.

14th row: As 2nd row.

Rep these 14 rows.

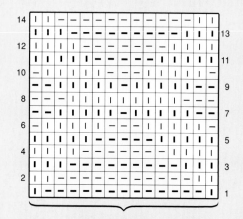

Rep these 15 sts

Zigzag Rib

Multiple of 12 sts + 13.

1st row (right side): P2, k2, p2, k1, p2, k2, *p3, k2, p2, k1, p2, k2; rep from * to last 2 sts, p2.

2nd row: K2, p2, k2, p1, k2, p2, *k3, p2, k2, p1, k2, p2; rep from * to last 2 sts, k2.

3rd row: P1, *k2, p2, k3, p2, k2, p1; rep from * to end.

4th row: K1, *p2, k2, p3, k2, p2, k1; rep from * to end.

5th row: K2, p2, k2, p1, k2, p2, *k3, p2, k2, p1, k2, p2; rep from * to last 2 sts, k2.

6th row: P2, k2, p2, k1, p2, k2, *p3, k2, p2, k1, p2, k2; rep from * to last 2 sts, p2.

7th row: K1, *p2, k2, p3, k2, p2, k1; rep from * to end.

8th row: P1, *k2, p2, k3, p2, k2, p1; rep from * to end.

Rep these 8 rows.

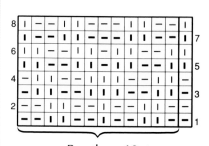

Rep these 12 sts

Maze Pattern

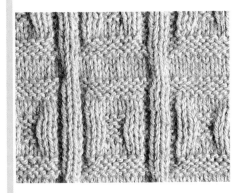

Multiple of 13 sts + 2.

1st row (right side): Knit.

2nd row: Purl.

3rd row: Knit.

4th row: P2, *k11, p2; rep from * to end.

5th row: K2, *p11, k2; rep from * to end.

6th row: As 4th row.

7th row: K2, *p2, k7, p2, k2; rep from * to end.

8th row: P2, *k2, p7, k2, p2; rep from * to end.

9th row: As 7th row.

10th row: P2, *k2, p2, k3, p2, k2, p2; rep from * to end.

11th row: K2, *p2, k2, p3, k2, p2, k2; rep from * to end.

12th and 13th rows: Rep the last 2 rows once more.

14th row: As 8th row.

15th and 16th rows: As 7th and 8th rows.

17th row: As 5th row.

18th and 19th rows: As 4th and 5th rows.

20th row: Purl.

Rep these 20 rows.

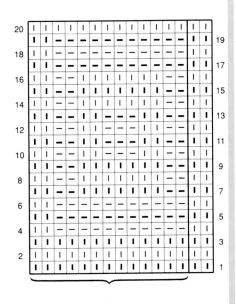

Rep these 13 sts

Broken Chevron

Multiple of 12 sts + 12.

1st row (right side): K1, p2, *k2, p2; rep from * to last st, k1.

2nd row: P1, k2, *p2, k2; rep from * to last st, p1.

3rd row: *P4, k2; rep from * to end.

4th row: *P2, k4; rep from * to end.

5th row: P1, k2, *p2, k2; rep from * to last st, p1.

6th row: K1, p2, *k2, p2; rep from * to last st, k1.

7th row: *K2, p6, k2, p2; rep from * to end.

8th row: *K2, p2, k6, p2; rep from * to end.

9th to 14th rows: As 1st to 6th rows.

15th row: [P2, k2] twice, *p6, k2, p2, k2; rep from * to last 4 sts, p4.

16th row: K4, p2, k2, p2, *k6, p2, k2, p2; rep from * to last 2 sts, k2.

Rep these 16 rows.

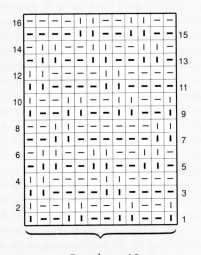

Rep these 12 sts

10(10-11) cm
[4(4-4½) ins]

52(56-62) cm
[20¾(22½-24¾) ins]

60(62-64) cm
[23¾(24½-25¼) ins]

8 cm
[3 ins]

BACK AND FRONT

48(53-56) cm
[19¼(21¼-22½) ins]

40 cm
[16 ins]

8 cm
[3 ins]

29(29-33) cm
[11½(11½-13¼) ins]

SLEEVE

Man's Cabled Sweater

Measurements

To fit chest size	85/90	95/100	105/110	cm
	34/36	38/40	42/44	ins
Finished measurement	104	113	124	cm
	41½	45	49½	ins
Length to shoulder	68	70	72	cm
	26¾	27½	28¼	ins
Sleeve length	48	48	48	cm
	19	19	19	ins

Shown in 105/110 cm [42/44 inch] size.

Materials

Aran knitting yarn	1100	1200	1350	grams
	40	43	49	ounces

Pair needles each size 4½mm (UK 7, USA 7) and 3¾mm (UK 9, USA 5).

The quantities of yarn stated are based on average requirements and are therefore approximate.
For abbreviations see page 24.

Tension

19 sts and 25 rows = 10 cm [4 ins] square measured over st st using larger needles.

Special Abbreviation

C4B (Cable 4 Back) = slip next 2 sts on to cable needle and hold at back of work, knit next 2 sts from left-hand needle, then knit sts from cable needle.

Back

Using smaller needles cast on 83(93-103) sts.
1st row (right side): K1, *p1, k1; rep from * to end.
2nd row: P1, *k1, p1; rep from * to end.
Rep these 2 rows until rib measures 8 cm [3 ins] ending with a right side row.
Next row (increase): Rib 4(2-3), *inc in each of next 3(2-2) sts, rib 1; rep from * to last 7(4-4) sts, inc in each of next 3(1-1) sts, rib to end. 140(152-168) sts.
Change to larger needles and commence pattern.
1st row: P3(4-2), k4, *p2, k2, p2, k4; rep from * to last 3(4-2) sts, p3(4-2).
2nd row: K3(4-2), p4, *k2, p2, k2, p4; rep from * to last 3(4-2) sts, k3(4-2).
3rd row: P3(4-2), C4B, *p2, k2, p2, C4B; rep from * to last 3(4-2) sts, p3(4-2).
4th row: As 2nd row.

5th row: As 1st row.
6th row: As 2nd row.
These 6 rows form the pattern. Continue in pattern until back measures 68(70-72) cm [26¾ (27½ - 28¼ ins] or required length to shoulder ending with a wrong side row.

Shape Shoulders

Cast off 45(50-57) sts at beg of next 2 rows. Slip remaining 50(52-54) sts on to a holder for neckband.

Front

Work as given for Back until front is 23(27-29) rows shorter than back to start of shoulder shaping thus ending with a right side row.

Shape Neck

1st row: Work 56(62-69) sts in pattern, turn and complete this side first.
Dec 1 st at neck edge on next 7 rows, then following 4(5-5) alt rows. 45(50-57) sts remain. Work 8(10-12) rows straight thus ending at side edge. Cast off.
Slip next 28(28-30) sts at centre on to a holder for neckband. With wrong side of work facing, rejoin yarn to neck edge of remaining 56(62-69) sts and work in pattern to end. Dec 1 st at neck edge on next 7 rows, then following 4(5-5) alt rows. 45(50-57) sts remain. Work 7(9-11) rows straight thus ending at side edge. Cast off.

Sleeves

Using smaller needles cast on 45(45-

49) sts and work 8 cm [3 ins] in k1, p1 rib as given for Back ending with a right side row.
Next row (increase): Rib 6(6-5), inc in every st to last 6(6-5) sts, rib to end. 78(78-88) sts.
Change to larger needles and commence pattern.
1st row: P2, k4, *p2, k2, p2, k4; rep from * to last 2 sts, p2.
2nd row: K2, p4, *k2, p2, k2, p4; rep from * to last 2 sts, k2.
3rd row: P2, C4B, *p2, k2, p2, C4B; rep from * to last 2 sts, p2.
4th row: As 2nd row.
5th row: As 1st row.
6th row: As 2nd row.
Keeping pattern correct and bringing extra sts into pattern, inc 1 st at each end of next row, then every following alt row until there are 104(126-136) sts. Inc 1 st at each end of every following 4th row until there are 130(142-152) sts. Work straight until sleeve measures 48 cm [19 ins] ending with a wrong side row. Cast off.

Finishing and Neckband

Press according to instructions on page 22. Join left shoulder seam.

Neckband

Using smaller needles and with right side of work facing, work across sts on holder at back neck as follows: K5(2-3), *k2tog, k2, k2tog, k1; rep from * to last 10(8-9) sts, k2tog, k2, k2tog, k4(2-3), pick up and k18(22-24) sts down left front slope, work across sts on holder at front neck as follows: K3, *k2tog, k2, k2tog, k1; rep from * to last 4(4-6) sts, k2tog, k2(2-4) and pick up and k18(22-24) sts up right front slope. 95(103-111) sts.

Starting with a 2nd row, work 8 cm [3 ins] in k1, p1 rib as given for Back. Slip sts on to a length of yarn.

Join right shoulder seam and ends of neckband. Fold neckband in half to inside and slip-stitch **loosely** in place, allowing for stretch and taking care to catch every stitch. Fold each sleeve in half lengthways and mark centre of cast off edge. Sew each sleeve to a side edge placing centre at shoulder seam.
Note: Armholes should measure approximately 24(26-28) cm [9½ (10½ - 11¼) ins]. Join side and sleeve seams.

Cable Stitches

4-Stitch Cable I
(on left of photograph)

Panel of 4 sts on a background of reverse st st.

1st row (right side): K4.

2nd row: P4.

3rd row: C4B.

4th row: P4.

Rep these 4 rows.

Panel of 4 sts

4-Stitch Cable II
(on right of photograph)

Work as given for 4-Stitch Cable I **but** working C4F in place of C4B.

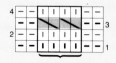

Panel of 4 sts

4-Stitch Cable III
(on left of photograph)

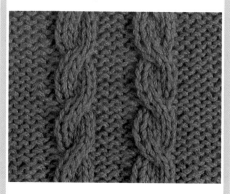

Panel of 4 sts on a background of reverse st st.

1st row (right side): K4.

2nd row: P4.

3rd and 4th rows: Rep these 2 rows once more.

5th row: C4B.

6th row: P4.

Rep these 6 rows.

Panel of 4 sts

4-Stitch Cable IV
(on right of photograph)

Work as given for 4-Stitch Cable III **but** working C4F in place of C4B.

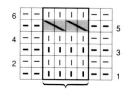

Panel of 4 sts

6-Stitch Plait I
(on right of photograph)

Panel of 6 sts on a background of reverse st st.

1st row (right side): K2, C4F.

2nd row: P6.

3rd row: C4B, k2.

4th row: P6.

Rep these 4 rows.

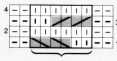

Panel of 6 sts

6-Stitch Plait II
(on left of photograph)

Work as given for 6-Stitch Plait I **but** working C4B in place of C4F, and C4F in place of C4B.

Panel of 6 sts

4-Stitch Snaky Cable

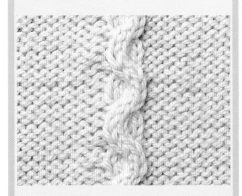

Panel of 4 sts on a background of reverse st st.

1st row (right side): K4.

2nd row: P4.

3rd row: C4B.

4th row: P4.

5th and 6th rows: As 1st and 2nd rows.

7th row: C4F.

8th row: P4.

Rep these 8 rows.

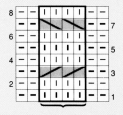

Panel of 4 sts

Double Snaky Cable

Panel of 8 sts on a background of reverse st st.

1st row (right side): K8.

2nd row: P8.

3rd row: C4B, C4F.

4th row: P8.

5th and 6th rows: As 1st and 2nd rows.

7th row: C4F, C4B.

8th row: P8.

Rep these 8 rows.

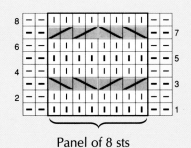

Panel of 8 sts

Honeycomb Pattern

Panel with a multiple of 8 sts. The example shown is worked over 24 sts.

1st row (right side): Knit.

2nd row: Purl.

3rd row: *C4B, C4F; rep from * to end of panel.

4th row: Purl.

5th and 6th rows: As 1st and 2nd rows.

7th row: *C4F, C4B; rep from * to end of panel.

8th row: Purl.

Rep these 8 rows.

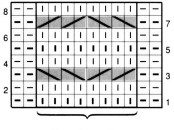

Rep these 8 sts

Cable Stitches

Oxo Cable

Panel of 8 sts on a background of reverse st st.

1st row (right side): K8.

2nd row: P8.

3rd row: C4B, C4E.

4th row: P8.

5th to 10th rows: Rep these 4 rows once more, then 1st and 2nd rows again.

11th row: C4F, C4B.

12th row: P8.

13th and 14th rows: As 1st and 2nd rows.

15th and 16th rows: As 11th and 12th rows.

Rep these 16 rows.

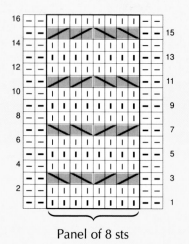

Panel of 8 sts

Tight Braid Cable

Panel with a multiple of 4 sts + 6. The example shown is worked over 10 sts on a backgound of reverse st st.

1st row (right side): K2, *C4F; rep from * to end of panel.

2nd row: Purl.

3rd row: *C4B; rep from * to last 2 sts of panel, k2.

4th row: Purl.

Rep these 4 rows.

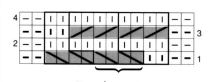

Rep these 4 sts

Claw Pattern I
(on left of photograph)

Panel of 8 sts on a background of reverse st st.

1st row (right side): K8.

2nd row: P8.

3rd row: C4F, C4B.

4th row: P8.

Rep these 4 rows.

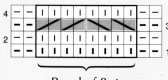

Panel of 8 sts

Claw Pattern II
(on right of photograph)

Work as given for Claw Pattern I **but** working C4B in place of C4F, and C4F in place of C4B.

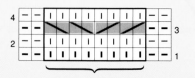

Panel of 8 sts

All-over Lattice Stitch

Multiple of 12 sts + 14 .

1st row (right side): Knit.

2nd row: Purl.

3rd row: K1, *C4B, k4, C4F; rep from * to last st, k1.

4th row: Purl.

5th and 6th rows: As 1st and 2nd rows.

7th row: K3, C4F, C4B, *k4, C4F, C4B; rep from * to last 3 sts, k3.

8th row: Purl.

Rep these 8 rows.

Doughnut Pattern

Multiple of 16 sts + 10.

1st row (right side): Knit.

2nd row: Purl.

3rd row: K9, C4B, C4F, *k8, C4B, C4F; rep from * to last 9 sts, k9.

4th row: Purl.

5th and 6th rows: As 1st and 2nd rows.

7th row: K1, C4F, C4B, *k8, C4F, C4B; rep from * to last st, k1.

8th to 10th rows: As 4th to 6th rows.

11th row: K1, C4B, C4F, *k8, C4B, C4F; rep from * to last st, k1.

12th to 14th rows: As 4th to 6th rows.

15th row: K9, C4F, C4B, *k8, C4F, C4B; rep from * to last 9 sts, k9.

16th row: Purl.

Rep these 16 rows.

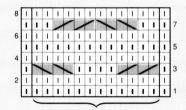

Rep these 12 sts

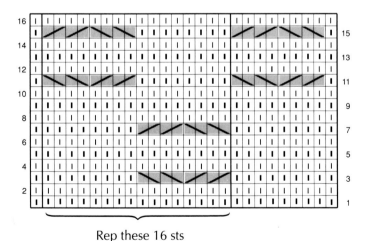

Rep these 16 sts

Refer to page 19 for
Step by Step instructions
for working C4B and C4F.

Cable Stitches

8-Stitch Plait

Panel of 8 sts on a background of reverse st st.

1st row (right side): K2, C4B, k2.

2nd and every alt row: P8.

3rd row: C4B, k4.

5th row: K2, C4F, k2.

7th row: K4, C4F.

8th row: P8.

Rep these 8 rows.

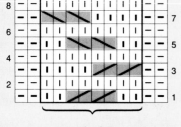

Panel of 8 sts

Double Twisted Cable

Panel of 8 sts on a background of reverse st st.

1st row (right side): K8.

2nd row: P8.

3rd row: [C4B] twice.

4th row: P8.

5th to 12th rows: Rep these 4 rows twice more.

13th to 22nd rows: Rep 1st and 2nd rows 5 times more.

Rep these 22 rows.

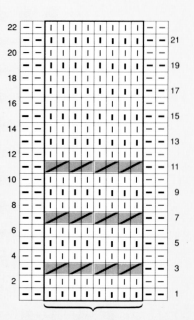

Panel of 8 sts

12-Stitch Braid Cable

Panel of 12 sts on a background of reverse st st.

1st row (right side): C4F, k4, C4B.

2nd row: P12.

3rd row: K2, C4F, C4B, k2.

4th row: P12.

5th row: K4, C4B, k4.

6th row: P12.

Rep these 6 rows.

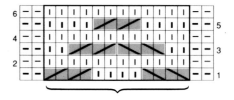

Panel of 12 sts

Staghorn Cable I

Panel of 16 sts on a background of reverse st st.

1st row (right side): K4, C4B, C4F, k4.

2nd row: P16.

3rd row: K2, C4B, k4, C4F, k2.

4th row: P16.

5th row: C4B, k8, C4F.

6th row: P16.

Rep these 6 rows.

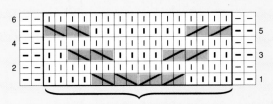

Panel of 16 sts

Staghorn Cable II

Panel of 16 sts on a background of reverse st st.

1st row (right side): C4F, k8, C4B.

2nd row: P16.

3rd row: K2, C4F, k4, C4B, k2.

4th row: P16.

5th row: K4, C4F, C4B, k4.

6th row: P16.

Rep these 6 rows.

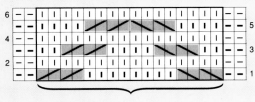

Panel of 16 sts

For information about working Panels refer to page 24.

Cable Stitches

Cable Squares

Multiple of 12 sts + 14.

1st row (right side): [P1, k1] twice, p1, k5, *p1, [k1, p1] 3 times, k5; rep from * to last 4 sts, [p1, k1] twice.

2nd row: [K1, p1] twice, k1, p5, *[k1, p1] 3 times, k1, p5; rep from * to last 4 sts, [k1, p1] twice.

3rd row: P1, [k1, p1] twice, *C4B, [k1, p1] 4 times; rep from * to last 9 sts, C4B, k1, [p1, k1] twice.

4th row: As 2nd row.

5th to 12th rows: Rep these 4 rows twice more.

13th row: Knit.

14th row: Purl.

15th row: K1, *C4B; rep from * to last st, k1.

16th row: Purl.

Rep these 16 rows.

Rep these 12 sts

Alternating Plait

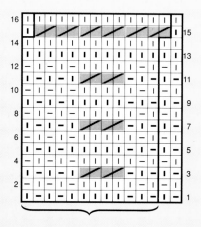

Panel of 8 sts on a background of reverse st st.

1st row (right side): K4, C4F.

2nd row: P8.

3rd row: K8.

4th row: P8.

5th and 6th rows: As 1st and 2nd rows.

7th row: C4B, k4.

8th row: P8.

9th and 10th rows: As 3rd and 4th rows.

11th and 12th rows: As 7th and 8th rows.

Rep these 12 rows.

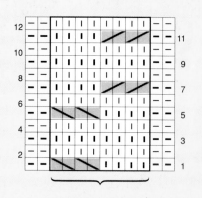

Panel of 8 sts